PRESIDENT'S MALARIA INITIATIVE

Ethiopia

Malaria Operational Plan FY 2015

Table of Contents

ACRONYMS AND ABBREVIATIONS

ACT	Artemisinin-based combination therapy
AL	Artemether-lumefantrine
ANC	Antenatal care
API	Annual parasite incidence
APS	Annual Program Statements
CDC	Centers for Disease Control and Prevention
CNHDE	Center for National Health Development in Ethiopia
DDT	Dichloro-diphenyl-trichloroethane
DHS	Demographic and Health Survey
EHNRI	Ethiopian Health and Nutrition Research Institute (newly named "EPHI")
EPHI	Ethiopian Public Health Institute (formerly known as "EHNRI")
ESR	Epidemic Surveillance and Response
FANC	Focused antenatal care
FBO	Faith based organizations
FELTP	Field Epidemiology and Laboratory Training Program
FMHACA	Food, Medicine and Health Care Administration and Control Authority
FMOH	Federal Ministry of Health
GHI	Global Health Initiative
Global Fund	Global Fund to Fight AIDS, Tuberculosis and Malaria (GFATM or GF)
GoE	Government of Ethiopia
HCMIS	Health Commodity Management Information System
HDA	Health Development Army
HEP	Health Extension Package (or Program)
HEW	Health Extension Worker
HMIS	Health Management Information System
HSDP	Health Sector Development Plan
iCCM	Integrated community case management
IEC/BCC	Information education communication/behavior change communication
IPTp	Intermittent preventive treatment of pregnant women
IRS	Indoor residual spraying
ITN	Insecticide-treated bed net
LLIN	Long-lasting insecticidal net
MCST	Malaria Control Support Team
M&E	Monitoring and evaluation
MIS	Malaria Indicator Survey
MNCH	Maternal neonatal and child health
MOP	Malaria operational plan
NFM	New Funding Model
NGO	Non-governmental organization
NMCP	National Malaria Control Program
NSP	National Strategic Plan
ORHB	Oromia Regional Health Bureau
PCV	US Peace Corps Volunteer
PEPFAR	President's Emergency Plan for AIDS Relief

PFSA	Pharmaceutical Fund and Supply Agency
PHEM	Public Health Emergency Management
PLMP	Pharmaceutical Logistics Master Plan
PMI	President's Malaria Initiative
PMTCT	Prevention of mother-to-child transmission
QA/QC	Quality assurance/quality control
RBM	Roll Back Malaria
RDT	Rapid diagnostic test (also called Rapid Test Kit or RTK)
RHB	Regional Health Bureau
SBCC	Social behavior change communication
SNNPR	Southern Nations, Nationalities and People's Regional State
TAC	Technical Advisory Committee
TFM	Transitional Funding Mechanism
UNICEF	United Nations Children's Emergency Fund
USAID	United States Agency for International Development
USG	United States Government
WHO	World Health Organization

EXECUTIVE SUMMARY

Malaria prevention and control are major foreign assistance objectives of the U.S. Government (USG). The purpose of this Malaria Operational Plan (MOP) is to provide a framework and a rationale for nominating and supporting malaria prevention and control projects in Ethiopia with Fiscal Year (FY) 2015 funding to accomplish the USG's foreign assistance objectives through the President's Malaria Initiative (PMI) in the context of the Global Health Initiative (GHI). Through the GHI, the USG will help partner countries improve health outcomes, with a particular focus on improving the health of women, newborns, and children. The MOP process for PMI Year 8 (FY 2015) considers information from the Ethiopian Federal Ministry of Health (FMOH), Regional Health Bureaus including the Oromia Regional Health Bureau (ORHB), international malaria program donors including the Global Fund to Fight AIDS, Tuberculosis and Malaria (Global Fund), malaria subject matter experts, and other malaria program stakeholders about the malaria situation, and the malaria control program capacities and gaps in Ethiopia.

The President's Malaria Initiative is a core component of the GHI, along with health programs for HIV/AIDS and tuberculosis. PMI was launched in June 2005 to rapidly scale up malaria prevention and treatment interventions and reduce malaria-related mortality by 50% in selected high-burden countries in sub-Saharan Africa. Other PMI goals include removing malaria as a major public health problem, promoting development in the Africa region, strengthening malaria control activities, and containing the spread of antimalarial drug resistance. The programming of PMI activities follows the core principles of GHI: encouraging country ownership and investing in country-led plans and health systems; increasing impact and efficiency through strategic coordination and programmatic integration; strengthening and leveraging key partnerships, multilateral organizations, and private contributions; implementing a woman- and girl-centered approach; improving monitoring and evaluation; and promoting research and innovation.

Over 50 million (60%) of the total Ethiopian population of 84.2 million live in areas at significant risk of malaria as of 2014, generally at altitudes below 2,000 meters above sea level. In 2014, the FMOH's National Malaria Strategic Plan (NSP) and Global Fund Concept Note (as of June 14, 2014) stratified Ethiopian malaria transmission risk within 835 districts both by population and annual parasite incidence per thousand as: High (>100/1000, 11 million (13%)), Medium (5 to 99.9/1000, 28.1 million (34%)), Low (0.1 to 4.9, 11.1 million (13%)), and Malaria-Free (0, 33.6 million (40%)). According to the FMOH, in 2011/2012, malaria was the leading cause of outpatient visits, accounting for 17% of all outpatient visits, and 8% of health facility admissions among all age groups. Malaria is one of the top ten causes of inpatient deaths among children aged less than five years and in older individuals according to Health Management Information System (HMIS) data. In 2012/2013, there were 57,503 public sector malaria hospitalizations, 4,984,266 malaria outpatient cases, 2,942,031 laboratory-confirmed *Plasmodium falciparum* outpatient malaria cases, and 1,258,131 *P. vivax* cases according to the annual micro-plan.

PMI support to malaria prevention and control in Ethiopia began in FY 2008 with an initial focus on Oromia Regional State, the largest of Ethiopia's nine regional states, covering a third of the country. PMI has contributed between $20 and $45 million annually to malaria control efforts in

Ethiopia during the last six fiscal years. In addition, Ethiopia has received four malaria grants from the Global Fund in recent years, with the most recent grant valued at $150,578,565 for the period of 2014 to 2016. With this support and that of other donors, the Government of Ethiopia (GoE)'s FMOH has been able to dramatically scale-up its efforts in malaria prevention and control in the last decade.

The most recent Malaria Indicator Survey (MIS), in 2011, showed that the prevalence of malaria parasitemia was 1.3%, and that long-lasting insecticide treated net (LLIN) ownership had dramatically increased from the baseline in 2000, but was still below target levels. Historically, Ethiopia experienced cycles of major malaria epidemics every five to eight years, with the last nationwide epidemic in 2003, associated with over 40,000 malaria deaths and affecting 211 of about the then 800 total districts. There have been comparatively fewer malaria epidemics since 2004 in Ethiopia, with reduced severity and mortality.

The activities PMI proposes with FY 2015 funding will complement the FMOH's current NSP for Malaria Prevention and Control, and build on investments made by the GoE and other partners over the past ten years. While a major focus continues to be on Oromia Regional State, PMI will continue to expand national-scope activities with FY 2015 funding. The proposed FY 2015 PMI budget for Ethiopia is $40 million. Outlined below are the FY 2015 budget's major components, which sustain and expand PMI support to most ongoing activities.

Insecticide-treated nets (ITNs) (Note: ITNs & LLINs are now essentially synonymous in Ethiopia): Between 2005 and 2014, over 64 million LLINs were distributed in mass campaigns by the FMOH nationwide, including 11.7 million LLINs purchased and distributed by PMI. Under the New Funding Model (NFM) for the Global Fund, the National Malaria Control Program (NMCP) is planning universal coverage of LLINs through mass campaigns in 2015 targeting all malarious areas. According to the gap analysis, the national requirement for LLINs is 29,584,492. The resources currently available from Global Fund Transitional Funding Mechanism (TFM) and PMI will provide 20,802,724 or 70.3% of the total requirement of LLINs, which includes 6.8 million LLINs using FY 2013 and FY 2014 PMI funds and 13.9 million LLINs using funds from the TFM. An additional 8,781,768 LLINs are being requested through the Global Fund's NFM to reach universal coverage rates. With FY 2015 funding, PMI will procure 3.2 million additional LLINs for distribution through keep-up campaigns. The LLIN distribution will be complemented by comprehensive social behavior change communication (SBCC) efforts to ensure that ITN use by the population is maximized.

Indoor Residual Spraying (IRS): Since 2008, PMI supported Ethiopia's long-standing and extensive IRS program through a comprehensive range of activities, including improved targeting and enumeration of areas for IRS operations, improved IRS commodity and insecticide quantification, procurement, distribution and storage systems, training and supervision of spray personnel and appropriate pesticide management, entomological monitoring, and environmental compliance. With FY 2015 funding, PMI will provide comprehensive IRS support by spraying approximately 480,000 structures in 26 districts protecting an estimated 1.23 million residents and will provide partial support to 34 graduated districts that previously had been fully supported by PMI. PMI also will continue to support building the capacity of the regional, zonal, and district-level vector control specialists to conduct basic entomological monitoring and improve IRS targeting and implementation as well as improve pesticide management.

Malaria in Pregnancy: Due to the generally low transmission of malaria in Ethiopia, intermittent preventive treatment of pregnant women is not a part of the national strategy. Universal ITN coverage is promoted, giving special emphasis and priority to ITN use among pregnant women, and prompt diagnosis and treatment of clinical cases when they occur. With FY 2015 funding, PMI will support improved malaria case management for pregnant women through an integrated approach to fever management at the community level provided by health extension workers (HEWs) and expanded access to high-quality antenatal care through health centers. Also, PMI will promote expanded and improved malaria in pregnancy case management services through safe motherhood and focused antenatal care pre- and in-service trainings for HEWs and midwives.

Case Management: PMI assisted the FMOH in updating the national malaria case management guidelines in 2012. These guidelines reinforced the importance of confirmatory diagnostic testing for all suspected malaria cases, with microscopy at the health facility level and rapid diagnostic tests (RDTs) at the community level. PMI will continue to help the FMOH update these national guidelines when needed. The most recently available micro-planning data revealed that over 92.1% of clinically suspected malaria cases had a laboratory test to confirm diagnosis (microscopy or RDTs), and the number of empirically treated patients has declined, with substantial avoidance of artemisinin-based combination therapy (ACT) wastage. The national guidelines also revised recommendations for severe disease management, promoting rectal artesunate for pre-referral treatment and intravenous artesunate for inpatient management. PMI has expanded support for quality-assured malaria microscopy diagnosis to 560 clinical laboratories and regional laboratories in Oromia, Amhara, Dire Dawa, SNNPR, and Tigray. PMI supports training and clinical supervision strengthening activities for HEWs in over 301 districts in six regional states. PMI also supports provision of supplies, training, supervision, and implementation of quality assurance/quality control (QA/QC) systems to improve the quality and accuracy of malaria diagnosis and clinical management of fever, while providing sufficient quantities of RDTs and ACTs to meet all requirements for Oromia and fill gaps in other regional states. PMI also periodically procures enough chloroquine, quinine, rectal artesunate, and intravenous artesunate to meet national requirements.

PMI is also strengthening the pharmaceutical management system, including procurement, warehousing, and delivery of malaria commodities, in line with the national Pharmaceutical Logistics Master Plan through the Pharmaceutical Funding and Supply Agency. PMI also is supporting the ORHB and its expanding system of HEWs to promote early care-seeking behavior and adherence to appropriate malaria drug treatment. PMI support also has been provided to the Ethiopian Food, Medicine, and Health Care Administration and Control Authority to ensure that all malaria products entering the country meet quality standards. In addition, PMI supports monitoring of therapeutic drug efficacy in two of the ten antimalarial drug efficacy-monitoring sites throughout the country.

With FY 2015 funding, PMI will procure and distribute 5.4 million multi-species RDTs, 220 microscopes, 2.6 million ACT treatments, 1.5 million chloroquine treatments (for treatment of *P*.

vivax), together with drugs for severe disease and pre-referral care. In addition, PMI's quality assurance activities will be expanded to additional laboratories in Oromia and to the remaining regional state reference laboratories.

Epidemic Surveillance/Monitoring and Evaluation: With malaria prevalence low and further decreasing in some places, improved data and information management for operations in Ethiopia, tracking both the focal malaria burden and the local status of malaria related commodities and operations will be of great importance. To improve routine surveillance, PMI is assisting the FMOH in the enhancement of the newly updated Public Health Emergency Management system together with the HMIS for routine collection and analysis of facility-based data.

With FY 2015 funding, this support will be sustained, together with efforts to monitor malaria morbidity, mortality, and availability of malaria commodities at the district level. This complements support for nationwide, district-level ('bottom-up') malaria commodities micro-planning to ensure that commodity procurements and distributions match district-level needs and are reaching beneficiaries. PMI will continue support for epidemiology, entomology, and drug efficacy monitoring at sentinel sites. With FY 2015 funding, PMI will continue to support three staff enrolled in the Field Epidemiology and Laboratory Training Program and will increase regular on-site support and technical assistance to the Ethiopian Public Health Institute, formerly Ethiopian Health and Nutrition Research Institute.

Operations Research: Beyond routine monitoring of heavily invested interventions (e.g., LLIN durability as well as drug and insecticide resistance), there is an ongoing need for additional operations research in the Ethiopian context given decreasing transmission and challenges associated with the case management of *P. vivax* infections. With FY 2015 funding, PMI will assess the feasibility of providing chloroquine prophylaxis to pregnant women diagnosed with vivax malaria and evaluate the impact of rolling out single-dose primaquine on falciparum transmission.

Social and Behavioral Change Communication: The Ethiopian Health Extension Program provides malaria prevention and control information and conducts SBCC activities in nearly all malaria-endemic communities. The Health Development Army supports HEWs to increase contact with each household through networking with between one to five households to deliver malaria messages. During 2014, PMI supported two local organizations to conduct SBCC at the community level in selected high-risk malaria areas in Amhara Region and Jimma Zone in Oromia Region using schools and religious institutions. With FY 2015 funding, malaria SBCC activities will be more integrated and coordinated with other health behavioral change communication activities such as the maternal, newborn, and child health and family planning and reproductive health programs. PMI will also continue to support two local Ethiopian organizations through an Annual Program Statement mechanism to build local capacity in malaria communications.

Health Systems Strengthening and Capacity Building: As one of the GHI Plus Countries, PMI in Ethiopia is fully aligned with the GHI principles of building country capacity and integrating across programs. PMI provides significant support to Ethiopia's Health Extension

Program that includes 38,000 HEWs staffing ~15,000 health posts that provide curative and preventive services for a range of health conditions, including malaria, at the community level. With FY 2015 funding, PMI will continue its support for integrated training and supervision of HEWs and for development of their capacity to detect malaria outbreaks in their catchment population. In addition, PMI and the President's Emergency Plan for AIDS Relief (PEPFAR) will continue to provide the majority of the support for implementing the Pharmaceutical Logistics Master Plan and strengthening Ethiopia's pharmaceutical management system. The PMI-supported initiative on micro-planning for malaria commodities is building capacity for forecasting commodity requirements and monitoring consumption at national, regional, and district levels. These skills can easily be transferred to forecast and monitor other essential health commodities. In addition, PMI support has helped to improve the capacity within Ethiopia to conduct entomologic surveillance and monitor drug and insecticide resistance. Lastly, PMI is leveraging support through PEPFAR to strengthen laboratory diagnosis of malaria, in conjunction with strengthening of laboratory capacity to diagnose tuberculosis and HIV infections.

STRATEGY

INTRODUCTION

Malaria prevention and control are major foreign assistance objectives of the United States Government (USG). The purpose of this malaria operational plan (MOP) is to provide a framework and a rationale for supporting malaria prevention and control projects in Ethiopia with fiscal year (FY) 2015 funding to accomplish the USG's foreign assistance objectives. Previously published MOP documents available on www.pmi.gov were used as references to develop this document for Ethiopia. Proposed President's Malaria Initiative (PMI) Ethiopia FY 2015 funding is contingent on USG official approval processes; any approved PMI FY 2015 funding will likely be unavailable for authorized expenditures until late 2015. The MOP process considers information from the Ethiopian Federal Ministry of Health (FMOH), international malaria program donors including the Global Fund to Fight AIDS, Tuberculosis and Malaria (Global Fund), malaria subject matter experts, and other malaria program stakeholders about the malaria situation, and the malaria control program capacities and gaps in Ethiopia.

The President's Malaria Initiative was launched in June 2005 as a 5-year, $1.2 billion inter-agency initiative to rapidly scale up malaria prevention and treatment interventions and to reduce malaria-related mortality by 50% in 15 high-burden countries in sub-Saharan Africa. The USG announced Ethiopia as a PMI focus country in 2007, supported by $20 million in PMI funding beginning in FY 2008. PMI support was initially targeted to malaria control activities in the Oromia Regional State, which at that time had about one-third of Ethiopia's malaria burden, population, and land area. Together with both Global Fund and PMI funding and the support from other donors and partners, the Government of Ethiopia's (GoE) FMOH has been able to dramatically scale-up its efforts in malaria prevention and control since 2005.

In May 2009, President Barack Obama announced the Global Health Initiative (GHI), a multi-year, comprehensive USG effort to reduce the burden of disease and promote healthy communities and families around the world. Through the GHI, the USG provides assistance to partner countries to improve health outcomes, with a particular focus on improving the health of women, newborns, and children. PMI immediately became a core component of the GHI, along with the USG's global health programs for HIV/AIDS (the President's Emergency Program for AIDS Relief, PEPFAR), for tuberculosis control, and for the USG's support for Global Fund. The USG closely aligned its support for PMI, PEPFAR, and Global Fund through various steering and oversight committees and with coordinated funding processes within the GHI framework. With passage of the 2008 Lantos-Hyde Act, funding for PMI was extended, and as part of the GHI, the goal of PMI was adjusted to reduce malaria-related mortality by 70% in the original 15 countries by the end of 2015.

The programming of PMI activities has been aligned to follow the core principles of GHI: encouraging country ownership and investing in country-led plans and health systems; increasing impact and efficiency through strategic coordination and programmatic integration; strengthening and leveraging key partnerships, multilateral organizations, and private contributions; implementing a woman- and girl-centered approach; improving monitoring and evaluation; and promoting research and innovation. In June 2010, the USG selected Ethiopia as one of the first eight 'GHI Plus' countries, involving comprehensive, multi-sectorial approaches to USG global health development including PMI's support for malaria control and prevention. Since 2011, PMI annual budgets for Ethiopia increased from about $30 million to approximately $40 million to allow more support for malaria activities beyond the borders of Oromia Regional State. Internationally, the USG's PMI program expanded to support several additional countries and regions beyond the originally funded 15 sub-Saharan African countries with high malaria burdens.

Over 50 million (60%) of the total Ethiopian population of 84.2 million live in areas at risk of malaria as of 2014, generally at elevations below 2,000 meters above sea level. In 2014, the FMOH's Global Fund Concept Note (as of June) stratified Ethiopian malaria transmission risk as follows within 835 districts by population (%) and by annual parasite incidence per thousand (API): High (>100/1000, 11 million (13%)); Medium (5 to 99.9/1000; 28.1 million (34%)), Low (0.1 to 4.9, 11.1 million (13%)), and Malaria-Free (~0, 33.6 million (40%)). According to the FMOH, in 2011/2012, malaria was the leading cause of outpatient visits, accounting for 17% of all outpatient visits, and 8% of health facility admissions among all age groups. Malaria is one of the top ten causes of inpatient deaths among children aged less than five years and in older individuals according to the Health Management Information System (HMIS) data. In 2012/2013, there were 57,503 public sector malaria hospitalizations, 4,984,266 malaria outpatient cases, and 2,942,031 laboratory-confirmed *Plasmodium falciparum* outpatient malaria cases, and 1,258,131 *P. vivax* cases according to the annual micro-plan.

Previous PMI MOPs for Ethiopia highlighted unique aspects of malaria in Ethiopia, including the PMI geographical focus; the community-level case management through the Health Extension Program (HEP); the importance of diagnostics given the presence of both *P. falciparum* and *P. vivax* each with distinct treatment regimens (artemisinin-based combination therapy (ACT), and chloroquine, respectively) according to current national guidelines; and the instability of malaria transmission and historical patterns of recurrent epidemics. There have been important updates to some of these elements in recent years.

Geographical Focus and Scale: PMI in Ethiopia primarily focused on Oromia Regional State during the first three years of program support. PMI commodity and operations support from FY 2015 funding will continue in Oromia. However, PMI support continues to expand nationwide by filling commodity gaps including ACTs, chloroquine, rectal artesunate, and injectable artesunate, rapid diagnostic tests (RDT), microscopes and laboratory supplies, and supporting planning, training, and use of strategic information. PMI will also continue to support case management through the integrated community case management (iCCM) platform while continuing to expect progress toward Millennium Development Goal 4. PMI continues to expand support for malaria laboratory strengthening activities to other regional states in cooperation with the Ethiopian Public Health Institute (EPHI).

Diagnostics and the Treatment of Malaria and Pneumonia: The HEP is a cornerstone of the FMOH's malaria control strategy. In recent years, the FMOH has refined its HEP strategy by supplying health extension workers (HEWs) with multi-species combination RDTs to identify and differentiate between the malaria species *P. falciparum* and *P. vivax*, and with stocks of chloroquine for the treatment of *P. vivax* (which was previously often treated with artemether-lumefantrine (AL)). Beginning in 2012, rectal artesunate has been supplied to HEWs for pre-referral treatment of severe malaria illness. In addition, HEWs have now been trained to treat suspected pneumonia cases with antibiotics such as cotrimoxazole, and to manage diarrheal illness with oral rehydration solution. These new tools are being sustained through iCCM and have the potential to greatly increase the HEWs' capacity for accurate differential diagnosis and correct clinical management of acute fevers at the community level.

Entomological Monitoring and Insecticide Selection: With support from PMI, Ethiopia has greatly expanded its capacity for entomological monitoring, including vector bionomic studies and testing for insecticide resistance in anopheline mosquitoes. A network of Ethiopian institutions and entomologists has been established to sustain and coordinate entomological monitoring, which will provide an evidence basis for decision-making on the use and deployment of indoor residual spraying (IRS) and long-lasting insecticidal nets (LLIN).

Epidemic Threats: So-called "epidemic years," periodically occurring every five to eight years have been the historical pattern of malaria in Ethiopia, with the last such epidemic years occurring in 2003-2004 when 211 of 700 malarious districts were affected with an estimated 41,000 deaths including 25,000 children under the age of five years. The highland fringes between altitudes 1,500-2,000 meters and the Rift Valley are particularly vulnerable to epidemics. Especially large malaria epidemics were documented in 1988, 1991-1992, 1998, and 2003-2004. Population movements including seasonal migrant workers, local flooding, and famine conditions, and emerging resistance to antimalarial drugs and insecticides may also affect local communities' risks for local seasonal malaria transmission and for malaria epidemics. Since 2005, as many as twelve district-level outbreaks have been reported annually, but in 2013, there were only three district-level malaria epidemics reported to FMOH, with very few associated malaria deaths. The absence of major malaria epidemics for an entire decade is unprecedented since the 1950s, providing evidence that the nationally scaled up malaria control interventions are having a favorable impact on malaria control and prevention in Ethiopia. The unstable malaria transmission in Ethiopia makes accurate, timely surveillance of paramount importance, since small and large scale epidemics continue to be health threats.

Integration of PMI Support and Ethiopian National Strategies: This FY 2015 MOP intends to support the updated National Strategic Plan (NSP) 2014-2020 as documented in the Global Fund Concept Note (version June 14, 2014), which indicates the FMOH aims to provide universal LLIN coverage to all persons at malaria risk (60% of the population or 50.6 million persons), and to selectively provide IRS coverage according to annual parasite incidence (API) as shown in the following table. Case management, malaria surveillance, and social behavior change communication (SBCC) services are to be provided to all 84.2 million Ethiopians.

Table 1. Malaria interventions by annual parasite incidence strata of districts with affected populations, Ethiopia, 2014 (Global Fund Concept Note, FMOH v. June 14, 2014)

Strata	API/1000 population	Elevation (m)	Population		Districts		Interventions					
			Total	%	No.	%	LLIN	IRS	LC	Case Management	Surveillance	IEC/ BCC
FREE	0	>= 2000m asl	33,639,639	40%	290	35%	-	-	-	x	x	X
LOW	>0 AND <5	< 2000m asl	11,153,499	13%	101	12%	X	X*	Wa	x	x	X
MODERATE	>=5 AND <100		28,410,564	34%	287	34%	x	-	Wa	x	x	X
HIGH	>=100		11,023,284	13%	157	19%	x	X	Wa	x	x	X
Grand Total			84,226,986	100%	835	100%						

*32% of low-risk population in highland fringe areas will be covered by IRS to ensure protection of this segment from anticipated epidemics. Wa: where applicable; LC: larval control; IEC/BCC: information education communication/ behavior change communication (data Sources: PHEM and micro-planning 2013)

MALARIA SITUATION IN ETHIOPIA

Malaria Transmission: Vector, Parasite, and Human Host Interactions

Anopheles arabiensis, a member of the *An. gambiae* complex, is the primary malaria vector in Ethiopia, with *An. funestus, An. pharoensis* and *An. nili* as secondary vectors. The sporozoite rate for *An. arabiensis* has been recorded to be as much as 5.4%. The host-seeking behavior of *An. arabiensis* varies, with the human blood index collected from different areas ranging between 7.7 and 100%. *An. funestus*, a mosquito that prefers to feed on humans, can be found along the swamps of the Baro and Awash rivers and shores of lakes in Tana in the North and the Rift Valley area. *An. pharoensis* is widely distributed in Ethiopia and has shown high levels of insecticide resistance, but its role in malaria transmission is unclear. *An. nili* can be an important vector for malaria, particularly in Gambella Regional State. Detailed information on the basic ecology and distribution of these vectors in Ethiopia is provided in the FY 2008 MOP. However, insecticide resistance among these vectors has become an important issue, with implications for vector control strategies.

Plasmodium falciparum and *P. vivax* are the major malaria parasites in Ethiopia, with several recent therapeutic efficacy trials documenting that artemisinin and chloroquine have adequate effectiveness for treating these pathogens, respectively. To date, major problems with emerging drug resistance, counterfeit or substandard antimalarial drugs have not yet been detected in Ethiopia.

Typical human and mosquito behavior results in most malaria parasite transmission occurring during nighttime hours within rural households in the lowlands or highland fringe areas of Ethiopia. Malaria transmission may also sometimes occur outdoors related to nighttime work or social activities, or may be associated with temporary overnight travel to other districts. Many Ethiopian communities have a "low" and "unstable" malaria transmission pattern that results in low host immunity and significant malaria risk after malaria infections, increased tendency for rapid progression to severe malaria, and propensity for malaria epidemics affecting all age groups. The epidemiology of malaria in Ethiopia contrasts with that of many other countries in Africa where malaria morbidity and mortality mainly affects young children.

Malaria Transmission: Seasonality, Weather, Geography, and Climate

In Ethiopia, the interaction of mountainous terrain with variable winds, seasonal rains, and ambient temperatures creates diverse micro-climates. Ethiopian weather is also influenced by tropical Indian Ocean conditions and global weather patterns, including *El Nino* and *La Nina*. When a micro-climate creates local puddles, flooding conditions, and warm ambient temperatures that persist for several weeks within a malarious area with low population immunity, the resulting *Anopheles* mosquito proliferation may cause focal malaria transmission to accelerate, sometimes explosively. In Ethiopia, malaria is highly seasonal in many communities, but may have nearly constant transmission in other areas; at the district level, malaria outpatient caseloads may vary several-fold from year to year in an "unstable" epidemic-prone transmission pattern. Peak malaria transmission occurs between September and December in most of Ethiopia, after the main rainy season from June to August. Certain areas experience a second "minor" malaria transmission period from April to June, following a short rainy season from February to March. January and July typically represent low malaria transmission seasons. Since peak malaria transmission often coincides with the planting and harvesting season, and the majority of malaria burden is among older children and working adults in rural agricultural areas, there is a heavy economic burden in Ethiopia.

Parasite Prevalence, Altitude Strata and Annual Parasite Incidence

The 2007 Malaria Indicator Survey (MIS) indicated that parasite prevalence (as measured by microscopy) in Ethiopia was 0.7% and 0.3%, respectively, for *P. falciparum* and *P. vivax* below 2,000 meters altitude. The 2011 MIS indicated that 1.3% were positive for malaria using microscopy and 4.5% were positive for malaria using RDTs below 2,000 meters, with only 0.1% prevalence above 2,000 meters elevation. *P. falciparum* constituted 77% of infections detected below 2,000 meters elevation. The 2011 MIS demonstrated a remarkable demarcation of malaria risk at an altitude of 2,000 meters, with a13-fold higher malaria prevalence at lower altitudes compared to higher elevations. There was essentially no *P. falciparum* detected by microscopy among persons surveyed within households having measured elevations above 2000 meters in the 2011 MIS.

In 2014, the FMOH updated the country's malaria risk strata based upon malaria API calculated from recent routine surveillance data from each district, with strata as shown and defined in Table 1 in the Strategy section. A malaria risk map from this API analysis is shown in Figure 2, showing areas with malaria transmission risk by API classified as High (>100), Medium (5-99.9), Low (0.1-4.9), and Malaria-Free (~0). Areas with the highest malaria transmission risk as stratified by district API appear to be largely in the lowlands and midlands of the western border with South Sudan and Sudan, with some other high transmission areas in or near the Rift Valley (that extends from the southwest of the country to the northeast). Many densely populated highland areas were newly classified as malaria-free according to API including the city of Addis Ababa.

Figure 2: Risk map of districts by annual parasite incidence, Ethiopia, 2014 (Source FMOH NSP, v. June 14, 2014)

☐ FREE (malaria free)

☐ LOW Transmission

▨ MODERATE Transmission

■ HIGH Transmission

Malaria Surveillance Systems and Malaria Trends

Ethiopia's health systems have been greatly strengthened in case management and surveillance capacity since 2004. In the 12 months between July 2011–June 2012, the FMOH's HMIS received malaria morbidity and mortality reports from 2,518 (80%) of the 2,999 public sector health centers, and from 116 (93%) of the 125 hospitals, representing both a five-fold expansion of health facilities and malaria reporting, and expanded primary health service coverage to 92% of the population. In the twelve-month interval from mid-2011 until mid-2012, HMIS reported 3,898,319 total outpatient malaria illnesses, 44,696 malaria admissions, and 2,173 malaria deaths from public health facilities that respectively represented 17%, 8%, and 9% of outpatient visits, inpatient admissions, and inpatient deaths from all causes for all age groups. For children aged less than five years, there were 722,539 malaria outpatient visits, 8,979 inpatient malaria admissions, but only 160 inpatient malaria deaths. These data indicate that more than 80% of the outpatient and inpatient malaria burden in Ethiopia is among adults and children at least five years of age according to HMIS health facility reports. The FMOH's Public Health Emergency Management (PHEM) system receives similar reports as the HMIS but also receives malaria health post data from district offices on a weekly basis; this PHEM surveillance system now reports 80% completeness.

The PMI-supported annual micro-planning survey provides even better completeness than both the PHEM and HMIS systems, with essentially 100% reporting from the 16,003 public health facilities in malarious districts with 57,503 malaria hospitalizations from July 2012 to June 2013. There were 4,984,266 total malaria cases, including 4,200,162 laboratory-confirmed and 784,104 presumed (i.e., clinically treated) malaria cases. There were 2,942,031 laboratory-confirmed *P. falciparum* outpatient malaria cases, and 1,258,131 *P. vivax* cases. The micro-plan reported

11,132,111 laboratory-confirmed cases out of a calculated total of 11,916,215 suspected malaria cases (suspected cases were formerly termed, "fever cases" per WHO).

Although malaria remains the leading cause of Ethiopian outpatient morbidity, and is among the leading causes of inpatient morbidity, it is declining as a relative cause of inpatient mortality, especially among children aged less than five years according to HMIS data. Access to prompt rational malaria case management including laboratory-based diagnosis in remote rural areas has improved dramatically over the last decade alongside surveillance systems that appear to be accurately and nearly completely documenting public sector health facility malaria morbidity and mortality. These credible surveillance data and health information systems will be essential to guide malaria control efforts more rapidly and accurately, and the interpretation of malaria trends should be easier in future years compared to the previous decade during the scale-up of malaria control.

ETHIOPIA'S HEALTH SYSTEM

Ethiopia operates under a federal system of government. Administratively, the country is divided into regional states, zones, districts (*woredas*), and communities/municipalities (*kebeles*) (see Figure 3*)*. There are about 835 districts with different levels of malaria risk in Ethiopia, with an estimated at-risk population of 50.6 million people as per the new stratification (see table 1 above). The best available proxy for local malaria transmission risk in Ethiopia is household altitude below 2,000 meters (above sea level), since malaria is rarely transmitted at higher elevations (unless there are weather abnormalities and widespread epidemics). Many districts have variable topographical features, with some households within communities located above and below 2,000 meters. Due in part to household locations at various altitudes and distances from efficient malaria vector breeding sites, malaria risk is unevenly distributed within many districts and *kebeles*.

Figure 3. Administrative regional states and zones of Ethiopia

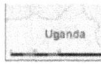

The health care service delivery system in Ethiopia has been re-organized into a three-tier system. The lowest tier is known as the 'Primary Health Care Unit', which is composed of one district hospital (covering 60,000-100,000 people), health centers (1 per 25,000 people), and their satellite health posts (1 per 5,000 people). The second tier is the 'General Hospital', covering a catchment population of 1-1.5 million people and the third is the 'Specialized Hospital', covering a population of 3.5 to 5 million people. The tertiary health care level is the third tier, comprised of Specialized Hospitals which serve an average of five million people. All the regional states including Oromia Regional Health Bureau (ORHB) follow the same health system. The health center provides comprehensive primary health care services and backup to the health posts by accepting referral cases, while district and general hospitals provide secondary health care. Health centers typically can provide inpatient services for up to two malaria patients, and they are equipped with injectable artesunate for severe malaria treatment.

According to the 2012/2013 Health Sector Development Plan (HSDP) IV Annual Performance Report, there were a total of 125 public hospitals, 2,999 health centers, and 15,668 health posts in Ethiopia. Oromia has a population of 32 million people with 304 districts organized into 18 rural zones and six zone level 'special towns' (Figure 4). According to a 2012/2013 report, there are 43 hospitals, 1,098 functional health centers, and 6,052 functional health posts operated by the GoE. There are also 8 hospitals, 5 health centers and 115 health stations under other governmental organizations (e.g., teaching or armed services hospitals). In addition, there are 3 private hospitals and 1,639 private clinics, among which 1,343 are lower level, 253 are medium level, and 43 are higher level. In Oromia, the health professional to population ratio is very low with 232 physicians (0.07:10,000 vs. WHO standard 1:10,000), but there is better nurse coverage with 9,757 nurses (3:10,000 vs. WHO standard 2:10,000). There are 12,875 rural HEWs and 692 Health Officers. There are a total of 3,207 available hospital beds (GoE 2,867 and non-governmental organization 340 hospital beds) with a bed-to-population ratio of 1:9,153 (WHO standard 1:3,000).

Figure 4. Administrative zones and districts of Oromia Regional State

The typical health post is staffed by two HEWs delivering 16 selected health packages, including one health package on malaria [http://cnhde.ei.columbia.edu/training/index.html]. Health extension workers are paid FMOH staff; they undergo one-year training after a high school diploma, and usually originate from the communities they serve. The HEWs focus on preventive services; however, they also provide curative health care services for malaria, pneumonia, and diarrhea using the iCCM approach of evidence-based diagnostic and treatment algorithms. For malaria, HEWs have been trained to confirm and report malaria diagnoses among clinically evaluated acutely ill patients using malaria multispecies RDTs. Severe malaria cases are to be referred to the next appropriate health facility, with initial stabilization with rectal artesunate. The HEWs are encouraged to consider other diagnostic possibilities for patients who test negative by malaria RDT, and to avoid empiric treatment with antimalarials when malaria RDTs are available. The HEWs are also expected to supervise seasonal health activities, including SBCC and mass vaccination campaigns, participate in surveys and a range of other community health activities. The HEWs work closely with the health development army (HDA) to perform these tasks. Additionally, HEWs have become more directly involved in supervising IRS spray teams and door-to-door mobilization for IRS. The FMOH envisages decentralizing IRS operations to the primary health care unit, where HEWs would be responsible for supervising the operations in their catchment area (*kebele*). Currently, the FMOH has started this practice in some districts in different regions and decided to scale it up in a stepwise approach.

ETHIOPIA'S MALARIA CONTROL STRATEGY

Under the framework of HSDP IV, Ethiopia developed a five-year NSP for Malaria Prevention, Control and Elimination (2011–2015), subsequently truncated to 2011–2014. The updated malaria NSP for the years 2014–2020 was finalized on June 14, 2014 and submitted along with the Global Fund New Funding Model (NFM) application. This strategic plan was developed following the MIS 2011 and the national malaria program review as well as in response to discussions and recommendations following a consultative meeting with key in-country and international malaria stakeholders as a part of the Global Fund's NFM. The following goals and objectives are set out in the new NSP:

Goals

- By 2020, to achieve near zero malaria deaths (no more than one confirmed malaria death per 100,000 population at risk) in Ethiopia.
- By 2020, to reduce malaria cases by 75% from baseline of 2013.
- By 2020, to eliminate malaria in selected low transmission areas.

Strategic Objectives

1.   By 2020, all households living in malaria endemic areas will have the knowledge, attitudes and practice towards malaria prevention and control.

2.   By 2017 and beyond, 100% of suspected malaria cases are diagnosed using RDTs or microscopy within 24 hours of fever onset.

3.   By 2015 and beyond, 100% of confirmed malaria cases are treated according to the national guidelines.

4.   By 2015 and beyond, ensure and maintain universal access of the population at risk to at least one type of globally recommended anti-vector intervention.

5.   By 2020, achieve and sustain zero indigenous transmission of malaria in 50 selected districts.

6.   By 2020, 100% complete data and evidence will be generated at all levels within designated time periods to facilitate appropriate decision-making.

The new NSP (2014-202) takes into account the findings of the 2007 and 2011 MIS, which showed substantial differences between the coverage and utilization of key malaria interventions by at-risk populations; community empowerment and social mobilization are therefore given high priority among the malaria control strategies in the new Plan. Similarly, malaria diagnosis, case management, disease surveillance and epidemic control are geared to serve Ethiopia's goal of shrinking malaria endemicity and achieving zero indigenous transmission in 50 districts by 2020. Accordingly, all malaria diagnosis is to be based on diagnostic testing, either by microscopy or RDTs, and treatment of malaria cases is to be guided by the result of the diagnosis. Surveillance will focus primarily on individual cases to identify the sources of infection and to limit further transmission.

PMI provided technical assistance to the FMOH to update the Ethiopian national guidelines for malaria diagnosis and treatment, vector control, and malaria epidemic detection and response, which are now available on the FMOH website under "important documents" by web-searching "national malaria guidelines Ethiopia." In 2013 and 2014, PMI provided substantial technical support to the FMOH in the development of the new NSP (2014–2020).

INTEGRATION, COLLABORATION AND COORDINATION

Maternal, Neonatal and Child Health, Family Planning, Reproductive Health

Following the first National Family Fertility Survey conducted in 1990, the USG started supporting the FMOH in the delivery of key Maternal, Neonatal and Child Health (MNCH), family planning, and nutrition services at the community level including expanded immunization, family planning, essential nutrition actions, malaria prevention, control and case management, promotion of antenatal care (ANC), and water, sanitation and hygiene. These interventions are delivered through health centers, health posts, and households and focus on rural, peri-urban, and hard-to-reach populations. To date, the program has trained over 60,000 community health volunteers, provided assistance to over 15,000 HEWs, and has reached over 32 million people (35% of the Ethiopian population) in 301 districts in eight of the country's nine regional states and parts of Somali Region. Under the Feed the Future Initiative, the USG will also continue to integrate health, agriculture, and humanitarian assistance and livelihood sector platforms to maximize impact on nutrition.

Most of PMI's support to these activities is being implemented through partners supporting the rural HEWs and the recently scaled up HDA at community levels with a multi-agency collaborative approach using GHI and United States Agency for International Development (USAID) processes and structures. PMI uses this platform to reach the most at-risk communities in malaria diagnosis and treatment, epidemic detection and response, and also to promote best practices in malaria case management by HEWs at health posts, including use of iCCM clinical algorithms.

PEPFAR, GHI, and other USG Programs

PMI is working with PEPFAR within the GHI framework through USAID and Centers for Disease Control and Prevention (CDC) structures, to harmonize the Ethiopia FY 2015 Country Operational Plan, with the USAID Health team's Operational Plan for tuberculosis and population health to ensure the respective plans complement and strengthen each other. Thus, currently approximately 20% of PMI's budget is allocated to so-called 'wrap around' activities with PEPFAR, i.e., either through co-funding of an award or by leveraging resources that have been established through previous PEPFAR support (e.g., laboratory infrastructure strengthening overlapping with HIV and tuberculosis diagnosis, malaria SBCC harmonization with other health messages, pharmacy system and supply chain strengthening). PMI also has important cooperative malaria ITN hang-up projects with U.S. Department of Defense Combined Joint Task Force-Horn of Africa and other malaria prevention projects with Peace Corps and CDC (i.e., Field Epidemiology Laboratory Training Program (FELTP), known as EFETP in Ethiopia) within the GHI context.

Coordination with other Partners

The Malaria Control Support Team (MCST) provides coordinated malaria technical support to the national and regional programs and is comprised of members of the FMOH, donors and international organizations, including PMI, governmental and non-governmental organizations (NGOs), and academia. The primary task of the MCST is to support the FMOH and regional health bureaus (RHBs) through ongoing technical assistance, resource mobilization, and support to epidemic preparedness and response. The MCST provides a common forum to share duties and responsibilities, avoid duplication and discuss priorities.

Part of the MCST is the Technical Advisory Committee (TAC), which includes the main malaria stakeholders in the country, i.e., FMOH, The Carter Center, Malaria Control and Evaluation Partnership in Africa, Malaria Consortium, PMI, UNICEF, WHO, etc. PMI is also a member of the TAC, representing a technical core of the MCST which advises the FMOH on policy and program implementation issues, providing technical assistance on an ad hoc basis, and assisting with malaria program integration issues. PMI has also been instrumental in the development and finalization of National Malaria Strategic Plan 2014-2020, five Global Fund proposals (Rounds 7, 8 and 10, Round 2 Rolling Continuation Channel, and Transitional Funding Mechanism (TFM)) as well as the recent NFM concept note, and the development and updating of in-country guidelines and strategies. Non-PMI funded malaria partners and other health donors as well as experts from the Global Fund were consulted to help develop this FY 2015 MOP document.

In addition, PMI is supporting coordination of malaria research stakeholders, academia and FMOH to fill the gap between the implementation of emerging malaria knowledge and research and the adoption of best malaria practices by researchers, practitioners, policymakers, and organizations involved in the prevention and control of the disease. Resolving this gap would serve to increase the benefits of quality research to improve prevention and control, and avoid duplication of efforts and waste of resources.

PMI GOALS, TARGETS, AND INDICATORS

Under the GHI, the goal of PMI is to reduce the burden of malaria (morbidity and mortality) by 70% compared to baseline levels in the initial PMI focus countries. Specifically, the reduction of malaria deaths among children under five years of age from a baseline of 2000-2004 is a major PMI goal while working in partnership with FMOH and many other partners. By 2015, PMI will have assisted the Oromia Regional State and the FMOH to achieve the following targets in populations at risk for malaria and targeted by activities supported by PMI:

- >90% of households with a pregnant woman and/or children <5 years of age will own at least one ITN;
- 85% of children <5 years of age will have slept under an ITN the previous night;
- 85% of pregnant women will have slept under an ITN the previous night;
- 85% of houses in geographic areas targeted for IRS will have been sprayed;
- 85% of pregnant women and children <5 years of age will have slept under an ITN the previous night or in a house that has been protected by IRS (note, because of the highly seasonal transmission of malaria in Ethiopia, one spray round per year is thought to be enough to protect the community);
- 85% of government health facilities have ACTs available for treatment of uncomplicated malaria; and
- 85% of children under five with suspected or confirmed malaria will have received treatment with ACTs within 24 hours of onset of their symptoms.

PROGRESS ON COVERAGE AND IMPACT INDICATORS

Malaria Indicator Survey 2007 and 2011

The 2007 and 2011 MIS assessed key malaria interventions, treatment-seeking behavior, anemia prevalence in children less than five years of age, malaria prevalence in all age groups, malaria knowledge among women, and indicators of socioeconomic status. For both surveys, field work was carried out during the high transmission season. The survey results were stratified by regional states and altitude (with communities <2,000 meters considered 'malarious'), and thus designated for FMOH targeting.

Table 2. Key malaria indicators reported in DHS 2005, MIS 2007 and MIS 2011, Ethiopia

Indicator	DHS 2005 National	MIS 2007 National (< 2,000 m)	National (≤ 2,500 m)	Oromia (≤ 2,500 m)	MIS 2011 National <2000m	Oromia <2000m
Percent households with at least one LLIN	3.4	65.3	53.1	41	54.8	43.7
Percent households with more than one LLIN	-	36.6	29.5	21.4	23.6	17.3
Percent children < 5 years of age sleeping under an LLIN the previous night	1.6	41.5	33.1	24.3	38.0	26.5
Percent pregnant women sleeping under an LLIN the previous night	1.1	42.7	35.2	25.6	34.7	26.7
Percent households reporting indoor residual spraying in the past 12 months	2.3	20.0	14.2	12.5	46.6	43.0
Percentage of households protected by at least one LLIN and/or IRS					71.7	63.7
Percent children < 5 years of age with fever in past two weeks	-	24.0	22.3	21.5	19.7	15.4
Percent children with fever who took antimalarial drugs	0.7	11.9	9.5	6.6	32.6	38.8
Percent who took an antimalarial drug same or next day	-	4.8	3.9	1.3	8.5	13.8
Percent children with fever who sought treatment from facility/provider same/next day	-	16.3	15.4	16.4	51.3	59.5
Malaria prevalence by microscopy *P. falciparum* (%)	-	0.7	0.5	0.1	1.0	0.2
Malaria prevalence by microscopy *P. vivax* (%)	-	0.3	0.2	0.2	0.3	0.3

Table 3. Malaria knowledge among eligible women age 15-49 years, Ethiopia

Survey	Region	Percent who have heard of malaria	Percent who recognize fever as symptom	Percent who report mosquito bite as cause	Percent who report nets for prevention
MIS 2007	National (< 2000 m)	79.5	50.8	41.1	38.2
	National (≤ 2500 m)	74.6	44.4	35.8	32.8
	Oromia (≤ 2500 m)	68.8	31.6	32.0	22.6
MIS 2011	National (<2000m)	71.3	76.0	71.2	63.4
	Oromia(<2000m)	68.7	71.3	73.2	65.5

The MIS 2007 results reflected the significant effort of the FMOH-led scale-up of malaria prevention and control interventions, with substantial increases in ITN ownership and use, as well as malaria knowledge. The 2011 MIS did not show incremental improvement in LLIN ownership or use compared with MIS 2007. However, the proportion of children seeking treatment for fevers within 24 hours (16% vs. 51% in MIS 2007 and MIS 2011, respectively) and women's malaria knowledge markedly improved. The percentage of people seeking initial malaria care from the public sector improved from less than half to 69%, indicating increased access to public sector health care. Tables 2 and 3 report national data for areas <2,000m and

<2,500m, whereas data reported for Oromia includes all areas ≤ 2,500m in 2007 and <2,000m in 2011. Protection with IRS increased from 20% to 47% between 2007 and 2011, and protection from either LLIN household ownership or IRS was 72% in 2011.

Both the 2007 and 2011 MIS showed the gaps in the scale-up of malaria interventions, clearly indicating needs for better targeting and a comprehensive SBCC approach to (i) maximize use of ITNs; (ii) maximize the efforts made in scaling-up IRS activities (e.g., by reducing refusal rates of households to be sprayed and decreasing the practice of replastering walls after IRS); and (iii) continue to increase access to malaria case management services.

A large sub-national survey of three large regional states (Shargie EB, *J Trop Med*, 2010) revealed declines in malaria prevalence from 4.6% to 0.6% between 2006 and 2007, suggesting that malaria program scale-up including ITN distributions might have been effective in reducing malaria prevalence. However, the 2007 and 2011 MIS in Ethiopia did not show significant changes in anemia and malaria prevalence.

Health Facility-Based Malaria Morbidity and Mortality, Ethiopia, 2001–2011

Otten *et al.* (*Malaria J* 2009, 8:14) analyzed health facility data from a stratified convenience sample of 13 hospitals within four Regional States immediately before and after malaria control scale-up. They detected declines in malaria outpatients, malaria inpatients, and malaria deaths of 81%, 70%, and 79%, respectively, in 2007 compared with baselines at these facilities from 2001-2006; however, this paper had several limitations including small sample sizes, data validity, and representativeness.

Jima *et al.* (*Malaria J* 2012, 11:330) analyzed Ethiopian Integrated Disease Surveillance Reporting system surveillance trends from the years 2005 through 2009 encompassing nearly all Ethiopian public sector hospitals and health centers. They calculated the national average of 23.4 total malaria cases per 1,000 persons (with two-thirds of these having been clinically diagnosed at that time). They reported malaria inpatient malaria admissions and malaria deaths averages of 6.4 per 10,000 and 2.3 per 100,000 per year, respectively. They reported that malaria inpatient admissions and deaths, including deaths from malaria with severe anemia, declined 2- to 3-fold from 2005 through 2009.

Maru *et al.* and WHO provided unpublished data to FMOH's draft NSP (June 14, 2014) about an analysis of 39 Ethiopian hospitals located at elevations below 2,000 meters from 2001-2011. This analysis of 39 hospitals revealed that: a) annual outpatient malaria cases peaked in these facilities in 2003 at 180,000 per year, then declined steadily through 2011 at 30,000 annual malaria outpatient cases; b) monthly malaria slide positivity rates declined to 15% in 2005–2011 from 23% in years 2001-2004; c) monthly malaria admissions significantly declined in 2005–2011 compared to baseline years 2001–2004; d) fewer monthly inpatient malaria deaths were observed at these hospitals from 2006–2011 compared to baseline years in 2001-2005.

Epidemic Detection Sites 2010–2013

PMI supported a network of ten sub-district malaria epidemic detection sites (see also Monitoring and Evaluation section and *Malar J* 2014 Mar 11;13(1):88) in March 2010 in Oromia Regional State, comprised of health centers and their satellite community-level health posts, and serving a combined catchment area of about 450,000 people. These featured weekly reporting of laboratory-confirmed malaria morbidity via weekly text messages from 83 health facilities, and a very high rate of laboratory testing for suspected malaria (i.e., with few, if any presumed, or clinical malaria treatments without laboratory diagnosis).

During the initial surveillance interval of 40 months since the system was established, 366,544 patients attended health services at these sites through June 2013; 47% and 53% of malaria outpatients were detected at health posts and health centers, respectively during the final 16 months between March 2012 and June 2013 when all health posts and health centers were reporting complete data. Of these, 152,803 patients were tested for malaria, and 37,438 (25%) of these had a confirmatory diagnosis for either mixed/*P. falciparum* (52%) or *P. vivax* (~48%) only, with children aged under five years comprising only 25% and 20% of these diagnoses, respectively, at health centers. Hospitalizations for severe malaria occurred in 0.3% (101/37,438) of those with confirmed malaria over the 40 months of surveillance with only two malaria deaths. Four sub-district level malaria epidemics were detected (using standard WHO criteria): two due to *P. falciparum* and two due to *P. vivax*.

From among these 10 sites, a single site, Guangua Health Center in Abaya District (population 35,000), experienced a sustained, predominantly *P. falciparum* epidemic between April and December 2011 with outpatient malaria morbidity that was more than three times higher than previous years (3,501 *P. falciparum*, 2,913 *P. vivax*, and 161 mixed infections) with 65 malaria hospitalizations and one malaria death. This single district-level outbreak comprised almost two-thirds of all hospitalizations (65 out of 101), and half of all deaths (1 out of 2 total deaths) experienced by the entire 10 sentinel site network.

Results of Malaria Program Impact Evaluation, Ethiopia, 2000–2012

PMI supported a comprehensive analysis of malaria program impact over thirteen years in accordance with the Roll Back Malaria Monitoring and Evaluation Reference Group (RBM/ MERG) guidelines in the context of substantial malaria control program scale-up since 2005. In Ethiopia, periodic national Demographic and Health Surveys (DHS) documented a decrease in all-cause child mortality per 1,000 live births according to survey year from 166 (2000) to 123 (2005) to 88 (2011). As previously mentioned, two key malaria indicators, anemia and malaria prevalence, were unchanged between national surveys in 2007 and 2011 during the midst of malaria intervention roll out, and adequate baseline measurements for these do not exist prior to 2005; this unfortunate situation prevented the typically recommended indirect causal analysis of malaria program impact through its effect on all cause child mortality per RBM/ MERG. Additionally, only about 20% of the malaria morbidity and mortality burden in Ethiopia is among children under five years of age. Nonetheless, relatively few malaria deaths have been reported compared to earlier years.

A direct analysis of program impact was made through triangulation of all available malaria data, including use of health facility-based data from newly strengthened surveillance systems, while accounting for the many possible limitations of this approach. Credible estimates of morbidity and mortality from the baseline period of 2000–2006 were at about 12.4 million annual malaria illnesses and 41,000 annual malaria deaths (51/100,000) among all age groups in Ethiopia (WHO World Malaria Report 2008, p. 69; and Negash K, *et al. East Afr Med J* 2005. 82(4): p186-92). The absence of periodic, severe, massive, multi-district malaria epidemics since 2004 in Ethiopia appears to have been attributable to the scale-up of malaria control activities. During this period, there were five-fold increases in health facilities and three fold increases in access to care within 24 hours of fever onset, indicating prompt access to effective malaria case management for the great majority of the most at-risk populations along with proportional improvements in surveillance. The coverage with LLINs and IRS increased significantly since 2005 to expect substantial program impact. The analysis of available evidence suggests that there has been at least a 70% decline in malaria mortality among children less than five years of age and among older age groups between the years prior to 2005 -when malaria program scale-up began- and 2010.

As of 2013, this malaria impact evaluation estimated that there were about 5.3 million annual malaria illnesses and 3,000-6,000 annual malaria deaths (5/100,000) among all age groups in Ethiopia, with 1,000 to 2,000 of these occurring among children aged less than five years of age. The updated NSP aims to reduce malaria deaths to about 600-1,000 annually among all age groups (1/100,000) by the year 2020; this ambitious goal for malaria mortality reduction can only be attained through continued government and donor support and the concerted action among many malaria partners in Ethiopia.

CHALLENGES, OPPORTUNITIES AND THREATS

Challenges

Programmatic challenges in malaria prevention and control include human resources gaps including shortages of appropriately educated and trained health professionals at all levels, and high staff turnover. PMI supports the Ethiopian FELTP that is designed to educate and train epidemiologists and laboratory personnel supporting malaria programs in Ethiopia. PMI also supports strengthening human resources capacity and the FMOH's Human Resources for Health (HRH) strategy through a specific project to train various health workers. PMI also supports district-level malaria program trainings using a WHO curriculum, integrated refresher trainings, and iCCM trainings per FMOH request.

Supply chain issues are an ongoing challenge. Ethiopia is a large country, with many remote areas with inadequate roads, providing challenges to delivering essential commodities to districts and to health centers and rural health posts especially during the rainy seasons. Pharmacy systems to detect malaria commodity shortages and stockouts need strengthening. The Pharmaceutical Funding and Supply Agency (PFSA) has been strengthened in recent years, and is actively supported by PMI's supply chain partners that continue to address gaps in logistics. PMI expects to work more closely in the future with PFSA through various supply chain partners to meet the FMOH malaria program needs.

Opportunities

The FMOH is committed to malaria prevention and control with especially high program commitment for the HEP. This is an important opportunity for malaria prevention and control since the HEP supports diagnostic testing and treatment for malaria, stabilization and referral of severe cases (including the use of rectal artesunate), LLIN distribution, and epidemic detection and response in remote rural areas with the most at-risk populations. Social behavior change communication activities are delegated increasingly to the HEP and to the new HDA that augments activities of HEWs in rural communities. Diverse elements of the Ethiopian public health system, academia, NGOs, and many other malaria stakeholders are committed to support the FMOH's effort in malaria prevention and control. The FMOH consults the Malaria Control Support Team's TAC and its subcommittees for most technical issues. The TAC had been involved in helping to draft proposals and concept notes for Global Fund grants and helping to ensure that PMI's support to FMOH integrates well with Global Fund malaria support in Ethiopia. PMI has several implementing partners, especially UNICEF, that are capable of procuring, importing, and distributing malaria commodities in a manner that harmonizes with FMOH's similar processes for Global Fund procurements.

Threats

Variable weather conditions, including *El Nino* and *La Nina* that affect seasonal rains, and global warming trends may fuel malaria vector proliferation with resulting focal and widespread malaria epidemics, and may also create famines and population migrations, including refugees from neighboring countries, possibly harboring novel malaria strains. In response, PMI supports activities to strengthen the PHEM surveillance system and HMIS that can detect and respond to epidemics. PMI also supports the FELTP, trained to investigate and help mitigate possible malaria outbreaks.

Currently, standard malaria treatment includes AL for *P. falciparum* and chloroquine for *P. vivax* infections. In Southeast Asia, antimalarial drug resistance has been well documented for these medicines. It is important to continue to document *in vivo* drug efficacy of these medicines and to provide an evidence basis for use of appropriate medicines for each malaria parasite species according to a laboratory-based diagnosis. The Food, Medicine and Healthcare Administration and Control Authority (FMHACA) has been supported by PMI to assess and maintain the quality of antimalarial drugs, and to prevent the importation or distribution of substandard or counterfeit antimalarial drugs.

Well documented insecticide resistance already threatens the effectiveness of insecticide-based vector control including IRS and makes such operations increasingly costly in Ethiopia. There are concerns that increasing insecticide resistance will reduce effectiveness of both IRS and LLINs. Alternative insecticides to pyrethroids are more costly, which makes maintaining existing coverage levels a challenge. Proper handling, storage, and disposal of unused insecticides pose occupational health, environmental impact, and logistical challenges. PMI supports ongoing monitoring of the emerging insecticide resistance situation to assist the FMOH and guide PMI IRS operations, and continues to promote best practices in insecticide use.

PMI SUPPORT STRATEGY

PMI's support strategy for Ethiopia has evolved since PMI began its activities in FY 2008, but remains consistent with the USG's PMI, GHI, and USAID global health strategies, and with country strategies within the US Embassy/Addis Ababa and USAID/Ethiopia. PMI's support to Ethiopia is in line with GoE's HSDP (2011–2015) and NSP for Malaria Prevention and Control (2011–2015), and the newly updated draft NSP 2014–2020 (and Global Fund Concept Note v. June 7, 2014). Since 2011, PMI has continued to support activities beyond Oromia Regional State, while maintaining a substantial presence in Oromia. Funding is targeted to fill gaps in activities that are not already supported by the FMOH, Global Fund, or other donors. PMI support has been flexible and responsive to the FMOH's evolving needs, including the occasional reprogramming of resources to provide critical malaria commodities that were not adequately funded by other sources. Additionally, PMI has provided considerable technical support and expertise for FMOH through malaria technical experts within CDC/Atlanta, USAID/Washington, the Global Fund, WHO, academia, and international development organizations.

OPERATIONAL PLAN

INSECTICIDE-TREATED NETS

National Malaria Control Program (NMCP)/PMI Objectives

The Ethiopia National Malaria Strategic Plan 2014–2020 recognizes the use of LLINs as a major intervention for malaria disease prevention in the country. The strategy is targeted to provide LLINs to all population groups living in endemic (high, moderate, and low malaria risk) areas to reach and maintain 100% ownership and utilization of LLINs (100% of households in LLIN targeted areas own at least one LLIN per 1.8 persons). Currently, all distribution of LLINs by the public sector is free of charge to the end users through the HEWs and/or health facilities. Ethiopia has distributed about 64 million LLINs since 2005. Usually, LLINs are distributed by periodic mass campaigns that occur about every three years in rotation using *woreda* level micro-planning data. The FMOH generally does not support routine ITN distribution by ANC or Expanded Program on Immunization clinics.

Table 4. LLIN distribution by different programs in Ethiopia (2005–2014)

Year	UNICEF	GF	WB	Carter Center	PSI	MDG	PMI	Total ITNs
2005	1,223,957	2,500,000	-	-	100,000			3,823,957
2006	354,750	3,825,500	-	-	300,000			4,480,250
2007	1,750,000	3,348,168	3,500,000	3,000,000	200,000		102,145	11,900,313
2008	-	778,423	1,600,000	-	-		22,284	2,400,707
2009	-	2,171,528	1,685,000	-	-		559,500	4,416,028
2010	180,000	11,350,000	114,600	2,958,897	-		1,000,000	15,603,497
2011	25,000	0	-	-	-	859,162	1,845,000	2,729,162
2012	-	1,000,000	2,700,000	37,295	-		2,540,000	6,277,295
2013	-	6,900,000	-	-	-	-	5,700,000	12,600,000
Total	3,533,707	31,873,619	9,599,600	5,996,192	600,000	859,162	11,768,929	64,231,209

The National Malaria Strategic Plan 2014–2020 proposes to use multiple LLIN distribution mechanisms to ensure all malaria-affected families are protected from malaria infection, which includes catch-up and keep-up campaigns. In the past, PMI LLINs have been used for keep-up campaigns to maintain universal coverage through sustained routine distribution of LLINs. In 2015, Ethiopia plans to implement a catch-up/mass campaign with distribution of LLINs to all targeted rural malaria-affected communities. The catch-up campaign is mainly handled by the HEP and local authorities. PMI has supported UNICEF, the Regional Health Bureaus, and the FMOH to jointly conduct annual micro-planning surveys since 2009. Micro-plan surveys collect malaria morbidity data, which is used for predicting annual malaria commodity consumption and forecasting commodity requirements (i.e., ITNs, ACTs, RDTs, etc.) for each village from the designated malaria district health official. The micro-plan results have also been used for new distribution or replacements of LLINs. The HEWs have been distributing LLINs for free to all households in all malarious areas, prioritizing vulnerable groups including pregnant women and children less than five years of age. The need for a mass campaign to raise LLIN utilization rates is noted nationally.

Ethiopia has seen a major improvement in LLIN coverage indicators from 2007 to 2013. The MIS 2011 showed significant improvements in LLIN household ownership in malaria risk areas from 3% in 2005 (DHS 2005) to 65% in 2007 (MIS 2007) and 55% in 2011 (MIS 2011). In areas below 2,000 meters, the proportion of children under five years of age who used an LLIN the previous night increased from 2% in 2005 (DHS 2005) to 42% in 2007 (MIS 2007) and 38% in 2011 (MIS 2011).

Progress During the Last 12 Months

Between FY 2007 and FY 2013, PMI procured a total of 11.7 million LLINs, which were distributed to malaria risk communities under a universal coverage approach primarily through the HEWs in Oromia Regional State. Since 2012, PMI LLIN distribution has expanded to other regions beyond Oromia focusing on high risk areas nationally. In 2013, PMI alone procured 5.7 million nets and distributed nets to high risk malaria districts in all the regions. The procurement of 3.3 million LLINs with FY 2013 funding is in process.

Distribution of LLINs for both PMI and Global Fund was based on a nationwide micro-plan developed by PMI in collaboration with the RHBs and other malaria partners in the country. The micro-planning exercise that PMI supported covers district- and *kebele*-level data on the number of malaria cases and key malaria commodities including LLINs. For LLINs, each annual micro-planning meeting compiles records of the number of LLINs previously distributed within the last three years, and documents LLINs that were more than three years old and thus need to be replaced. The micro-plan estimates the 12-month need and gap of LLINs based on district-level sub-populations with malaria risk (generally by *kebele*), malaria morbidity, and LLIN data. In addition to replacement of LLINs, the number of "gap filling" nets was calculated by quantifying the number of new households (resulting from population growth rates) and malaria-affected households that never received nets in previous distributions. The micro-planning process has now been adopted by other regional states and has helped streamline and coordinate the commodity procurement and distribution process as well as allowing tracking and prioritization of commodity distributions.

The FMOH plan to use Global Fund Round 8 Phase 2 and TFM funding to procure ~14 million nets in 2014 was delayed due to unforeseen reasons; by late 2014, most LLINs in Ethiopia will be reaching the end of their expected service life. The FMOH's Global Fund NFM proposal of June 14, 2014 (NFM Table 2) identified the need for 29,584,492 standing nets in 2015, as shown in Table 5. It is now assumed that most Global Fund procured LLINs (13,993,033 plus 8,781,768) will be delivered in late 2014 or in 2015 (Table 5).Since there are no other donor-procured additional LLIN other than PMI procured nets in 2014 due to Global Fund procurement delays, the NMCP is planning LLIN mass campaigns in 2015 targeting universal coverage in all malarious areas. The gap analysis conducted under Global Fund NFM estimates a total of 29,584,492 LLINs are required to achieve universal coverage. The resources available from TFM (13.9 million LLINs) and PMI (FY 2013 and FY 2014 funding 6.8 million LLINs) will provide 20,802,724 (70.3%) of the total requirement of LLINs (Table 5).

Table 5. LLIN gap analysis, 2015-2017

Year	2015	2016	2017
Population targeted for net coverage	53,252,086	54,636,640	56,057,192
National target *(from strategic plan) % coverage FMOH NFM June 14, 2014 Table 2*	100%	100%	100%
LLINs needed to cover target population	29,584,492	30,353,689	31,142,885
Total number of LLINs required (campaign in 2015 and keep-up in 2016)	**29,584,492**	**3,135,956**	**6,956,971**
PMI LLINs	6,809,691*	3,200,000**	3,200,000
GF LLINs (TFM)	13,993,033	0	0
GF LLINs (NFM)	8,781,768	0	0
LLINs available (all sources)	**29,584,492**	**3,200,000**	**3,200,000**
Remaining LLIN gap	**0**	**64,044**	**3,756,971**

Note: *PMI LLINs 6,809,691 in 2015 were procured with FY 2013 (3,300,000) and FY 2014 (3,509,691) funding. **PMI LLINs in 2016 is for keep-up campaign.

The FMOH expects the Global Fund NFM to cover the remaining 8,781,768 LLINs needed in the first year of implementation. The FMOH believes that this mass campaign will establish a foundation for the beginning of continuous distribution efforts that will require 3,135,956 LLINs to be replaced in 2016 and 6,956,971 in 2017 under keep-up campaigns. The NFM states that given no local evidence for loss rates of nets, the continuous distribution calculated nets lost based on the RBM Harmonization Working Group recommendation of 8%, 20%, and 50% in the first, second, and third year of distribution, respectively. There is a plan to generate local evidence on net loss during the implementation of the concept note. (Reference: NFM Concept Note, v. June 14, 2014)

Plans and Justification

PMI supports the FMOH policy and distribution plans of LLINs to the most at-risk communities in high malaria transmission areas as per NSP 2014–2020 malaria stratification. In addition to the LLIN procurement and distribution, PMI in collaboration with the FMOH and other in-country stakeholders are currently assisting with the national micro-planning process for the LLIN needs assessment and the plans for distribution. The FMOH requested, via the Global Fund TFM grant application, for 100% LLIN coverage of the at-risk population assuming one net for every 1.8 persons in 2015 and replacing LLINs after three years. In earlier FMOH grant applications, either two LLIN nets per household (averaging five persons) or one net per two persons had been requested. That policy was then later changed to one LLIN per 1.8 persons (the total population at risk divided by 1.8).

Proposed Activities with FY 2015 Funding ($13,280,000):

• **Procurement and distribution of LLINs to districts ($12,800,000):** Due to the pressing need to cover the LLIN gap, PMI will increase its support for procurement and distribution of 3.2 million LLINs in the keep-up campaigns to high malaria transmission areas nationally. The LLINs will be delivered to the district level and distributed for free to communities mainly through HEWs.

• **LLIN distribution from districts to health posts/communities ($480,000):** PMI will assist districts to transport LLINs from the district level to health posts and communities, at approximately $0.15/net. All activities will be coordinated with local authorities in order to ensure that engagement of targeted districts is maximized, LLINs are distributed before the malaria transmission season and communities are educated to use nets properly and to take care of and repair the nets appropriately.

INDOOR RESIDUAL SPRAYING

NMCP/PMI Objectives

Indoor residual spraying was first implemented in Ethiopia in the mid-1960s and has remained a key component of the national malaria prevention and control strategy since that time. In the NSP for Malaria Prevention and Control in Ethiopia 2011–2014, IRS was given high priority as a main component of vector control. Further, the objective of vector control in the new draft NSP (2014–2020) is "to ensure and maintain universal access of the population at risk to at least one type of globally recommended anti-vector intervention by 2015" and the IRS specific objective is "to increase and maintain IRS coverage to 100% of IRS-targeted districts/*woredas* by 2020." According to the FMOH's new NSP malaria stratification based upon API, only 31% of the districts in the country will be eligible for IRS (specifically highland fringe areas where the risk of malaria is low but with higher risk of epidemics and areas at lower altitudes with high malaria burden). Due to the varied topography and heterogeneous malaria transmission within districts, not all communities in a specific district will be targeted for spraying. Specific IRS-targeted communities are selected based on malaria case loads, altitude, presence of nearby *Anopheles* breeding sites, agriculture and water development practices, epidemic records, and other economic or social factors. The selection of communities for IRS will be refined every year from the IRS targeted districts. Successful implementation of IRS following the new stratification requires strong advocacy and training of managers and health personnel at different levels. Malaria transmission in Ethiopia is seasonal, lasting for about three months, mostly peaking after the main rainy season. Depending on the residual life of the insecticide used and timing of spray operations, one spray round per year could give the required protection against malaria.

Progress During the Last 12 Months

The PMI-supported IRS program in Ethiopia has expanded significantly from its initial 316,000 structures in 2008, reaching a peak of 858,657 structures sprayed in 2011 (Figure 5; Table 6). Since 2008, PMI provided targeted IRS to highest malaria burden *kebeles* (villages) in PMI supported districts according to the National Guidelines. In 2013, 635,528 structures in 36 districts were sprayed and 1,629,958 people were protected through PMI support. On the other hand, the FMOH has conducted spraying in 538 districts covering 8,125,401 structures and protecting more than 19.7 million people. The insecticide used in PMI-supported districts in 2013 was bendiocarb while the FMOH used both bendiocarb and propoxur.

Figure 5. IRS results in PMI-supported districts of Oromia Region, Ethiopia, 2008–2013

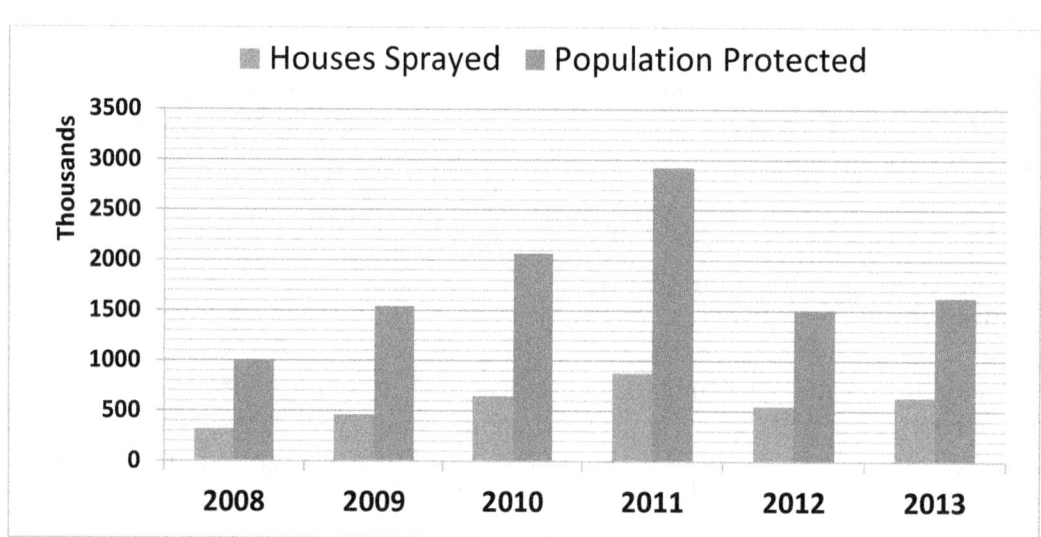

Table 6. PMI-supported IRS, 2008–2016

Year	Number of Districts Sprayed	Insecticide Used	Number of Structures Sprayed	Coverage Rate	Population Protected
2008	19	DDT	316,829	91.96	1,000,526
2009	23	DDT	459,402	91.8	1,539,163
2010	30	Deltamethrin	646,870	96.5	2,064,389
2011	50	Deltamethrin + Bendiocarb	858,657	98.64	2,920,469
2012	36	Deltamethrin + Bendiocarb	547,421	98.8	1,506,273
2013	36	Bendiocarb	635,528	99.6	1,629,958
2014*	36	Bendiocarb	635,528		1,629,958
2015*	33	TBD (likely long-acting OP)	597,714		1,532,975
2016*	26	TBD (likely long-acting OP)	483,170		1,239,201

*Estimates based on draft plans

District Graduation: In 2013, PMI continued providing two levels of support to districts following a system that began in 2012. Of the 60 districts supported, 24 districts were considered "graduated" and received minimal support, while 36 districts received full support from PMI, comprising of procurement of insecticide, operational funds, transportation, rehabilitation of district storage facilities, soak pits, personal protective equipment, environmental compliance, information education communication (IEC) and social mobilization, training on IRS techniques, and use and maintenance of spray pumps. Graduated districts receive only minimal PMI support, including micro-planning consultations, a limited supply of equipment, and technical assistance including environmental compliance monitoring, IRS operations micro-planning, and supportive supervision. The rationale for this graduation approach is that as districts build capacity through extended PMI support over two to three years, it is believed that they will be able to sustain IRS operations with their own resources and less assistance, with the funds saved being used to provide greater support to IRS in other districts.

According to a PMI-supported IRS rapid assessment in 2012, all 24 graduated districts had conducted IRS operations with support from the government and local NGOs, covering 428,459 structures, which represents over 82% coverage in the targeted communities. Further, in 2013, the graduated districts continued IRS of selected communities and maintained the 2012 level. In the event that district councils of graduated districts fail to allocate funds and IRS operations are disrupted in high transmission risk areas, PMI will advocate that the FMOH and RHBs intervene.

Community-Based IRS: The involvement of HEWs in IRS as part of the community-based IRS strategy is indicated in the NSP 2011–2013. Further, the draft 2014–2020 NSP underscores expanding the use of the HEP in the implementation of IRS. This was also elaborated in the national malaria prevention and control guidelines (FMOH 3rd edition, 2012). In 2012, the FMOH requested PMI support to pilot the feasibility of integrating IRS into the existing HEP and decentralizing the organization of spray operations from the district to the community level in one district, with a focus on ensuring environmental compliance, quality of IRS operations, and building the local capacity. Under this model, HEWs serve as IRS squad leaders and assume responsibility for managing store rooms, washers, and spray operators, as well as data collection and reporting. Spray operators are hired from same communities/kebeles and do not require transport and camping facilities. PMI's community-based IRS districts receive the full PMI package of comprehensive support, similar to PMI's district-based IRS and are closely supervised by the head of the District Health Office, the malaria focal person, and the environmental compliance officer, which each provide technical back-up when required. Based on the positive results from the 2012 pilot, PMI expanded community-based IRS to six districts in 2013 to assess this IRS method in a larger, more scaled up setting. PMI worked to ensure that a comprehensive evaluation was carried out that addressed the quality of spraying, logistical management, proper storage, handling, and disposal of insecticides, and the financial costs of such an approach. In areas with community-based IRS in 2013, 99.8% of eligible structures were sprayed. The 2013 community-based IRS evaluation report shows cost per person protected in the community-based model was about 24% less compared to the 2012 district-based IRS operations. Further the quality of spray evaluated by wall bioassay test shows no difference between both approaches. These six districts will continue conducting community-based IRS in 2014 followed by an evaluation to inform decision-making.

Resistance Monitoring: The FMOH acknowledges that a long-term insecticide resistance strategy is crucial to ensure continued efficacy of IRS in Ethiopia and has delegated EPHI to take the necessary steps in the development of the national strategy for insecticide resistance management by involving a range of stakeholders. Considering the rapid spread of insecticide resistance among malaria vectors in Ethiopia, the FMOH emphasizes the importance of continuous monitoring of insecticide resistance in the new draft NSP.

In 2013, PMI continued supporting entomological monitoring of resistance to 11 insecticides from four insecticide classes in five sentinel sites and mosquito behavior studies in three sites. The insecticide resistance monitoring results show that local vectors are resistant to DDT, pyrethroids, and malathion, which is consistent with previous years' results. It further shows possible bendiocarb resistance in some places which needs close attention. The insecticide resistance studies provide trends in the insecticide resistance status over time corresponding to changes in the application of different IRS insecticides following shifts in the insecticide policy of the country. In 2015, three sentinel sites will be added to fill gaps in national insecticide resistance monitoring. These sites will be in Tigray, Afa,r and Gambella. Insecticide resistance tests from the five fixed PMI and two other non-PMI sites are presented in Table 7. An indication of higher level of susceptibility to DDT, malathion, and deltamethrin was observed in 2013 compared to 2012 in most of the sites.

Table 7. Summary of PMI-supported insecticide resistance tests in 2013

		Mortality (%)					
		PMI sites				Other sites	
Insecticide class	Insecticide	Omonada	Zwai	Chewaka	Bahirdar	Ameya	Wonchi
Organochlorine	DDT	9	26	22	16	2	4
Pyrethroid	Permethrin	22				12	19
	Deltamethrin	26	36	51	20	16	23
	Lambdacyhalothrin	15		44		9	18
	Alphacypermethrin		32		43		
	Etofenprox		20		55		
Organophosphate	Fenitrothion	97		100	100	100	100
	Malathion	81	90	71	33	60	88
	Pirimiphos methyl	100	100	100	100	100	100
Carbamate	Propoxur	98.1	100	100	96	100	100
	Bendiocarb	92	100	100	75	100	100

Other entomological monitoring: In 2013, monitoring was conducted in two IRS operation areas using bendiocarb and one control site, using pyrethrum spray catches. *An. gambiae s.l.* density was significantly reduced in the IRS sites, compared with the control site; however, collections in all sites were low two months after the date of the spray. Over 60% of mosquitoes from human landing catches were collected outdoors and early evening biting was also detected.

Carbamate Residual Efficacy Studies: The residual life of bendiocarb and propoxur was evaluated on different wall surfaces in 2013, to better understand the factors that affect residual efficacy of carbamates due to the varying results seen in the Ethiopia program and across PMI focus countries (see Table 8).

Table 8. Residual efficacy of carbamates sprayed on different surfaces

Sprayed with	Types of walls	Time post-spray						
		24 hours	1 month	2 months	3 months	4 months	5 months	6 months
Bendiocarb (0.4g/m^2)	Painted	100	100	100	100	100	100	100
	Dung plastered	100	63.3	55.6	22.2	7.1	0.4	1.3
	Mud, wetted water	100	66.7	0	15.2	2.2	6.7	9.4
	Mud plastered	100	66.7	4.4	4.4	6.7	16.3	9.7
Propoxur (2g/m^2)	Painted	100	100	100	100	100	100	100
	Dung plastered	100	100	100	100	100	92.8	92.9
	Mud, wetted water	100	93.3	100	100	100	100	100
	Mud plastered	100	81	100	100	100	95.3	100
Local water	Painted	0	0	0	2.2	0	6.1	3.3
	Dung plastered	0	3.3	0	0	2.3	2.9	0
	Mud, wetted water	0	3.3	0	0	0	2.5	6.7
	Mud plastered	0	0	4.4	6.7	6.7	0	3.3

While bendiocarb and propoxur resulted in 100% mortality of susceptible mosquitoes exposed in cone bioassays for at least six months on painted walls, the results for other surfaces was much less encouraging. For walls plastered with dung or mud (which is the case in most rural settings of Ethiopia) and treated with bendiocarb, only 67% of mosquitoes were dying after one month and no effect was found after two months.

Strengthening National Entomological Monitoring Capacity: Building the capacity of district health offices to carry out key entomological monitoring activities as part of their annual malaria intervention plan is considered a crucial step in sustaining this effort. Staff trained in insecticide resistance testing in 2012 received a follow-up training on the CDC bottle bioassay in November 2013. These staff have already begun conducting the bioassays and submitting their results to the FMOH.

Numerous studies have shown high levels of mosquito resistance to DDT, pyrethroids, and malathion. The use of insecticides other than DDT and pyrethroids will increase the cost of IRS dramatically which will hinder the program's ability to sustain coverage due to the limited funding available. Epidemiological targeting of IRS to have the most impact; ensuring sustainability of the program; best use of the limited portfolio of resources; decreased efficacy due to existing wall structures and re-plastering of houses after spraying; the need to improve pesticide management, and meeting standard environmental compliance are areas that need more attention in IRS. PMI is working on the long-standing obsolete DDT removal from PMI-supported districts. Nationwide there are about 1,300 tons of obsolete insecticide (over 99%

DDT), most of it pre-dating PMI, in more than 500 districts that were managed by the FMOH and Regional Health Bureaus. With the USG's interest in protecting environmental and human health in Ethiopia, PMI supported an assessment to establish an inventory of obsolete insecticides at the district, zonal, and regional levels in the 60 districts where PMI currently or previously supported IRS. Different options for the obsolete insecticides' final disposal were discussed with the FMOH, ORHB, and other parties including the African Stockpile Program at the World Bank. A proposal to collect and ship 80 tons of DDT from PMI-supported districts was approved by PMI, USAID/Ethiopia and the Bureau of Environment environmental officers in April 2014. This activity would include repackaging the obsolete insecticide and cleaning the various stores that have housed the DDT for safety purposes. Local Ethiopian workers would be trained to undertake this activity, which will be an important resource in the future should the FMOH decide to act on the remaining DDT stores outside of PMI's districts. During the FY 2015 MOP visit, the Minister of Health gave his verbal approval to proceed with the proposal.

Plans and Justification

With FY 2015 funds, PMI will maintain the FY 2014 level of IRS support by working closely with the FMOH, ORHB, and other partners. In collaboration with ORHB, PMI will restart implementation of the graduation process with three low malaria burden districts in 2015 and in 2016 seven more districts are expected to graduate. Prior to graduation, preparatory activities including evaluation of the districts' technical preparedness in IRS operations, consensus building discussions, and securing adequate funding from the district council will take place with adequate lead time in collaboration with ORHB and implementing partners. The continuation or expansion of community-based IRS will be based on the results from the 2013 and 2014 evaluations. With FY 2015 funding, approximately 480,000 structures will be sprayed with full support from PMI in 26 districts, protecting a population of approximately 1.2 million people. In addition, PMI will provide limited support for IRS operations in the 34 graduated districts. PMI will continue to focus on high malaria burden districts in Oromia and support environmental compliance activities, entomological monitoring in sentinel sites and insecticide resistance testing.

Table 9. Planned IRS graduation of districts

	FY 2013	FY 2014	FY 2015
Number of graduating districts	None	3	7
Number of project districts	36	33	26
Structures sprayed	635,528	597,714	483,170
Population protected	1,629,958	1,532,975	1,239,201

Proposed Activities with FY 2015 Funding ($8,831,300):

• Indoor residual spray operations, training, and procurement of insecticide ($8,250,000):
PMI will continue to support ORHB in planning, implementation and evaluation of IRS in Oromia. With FY 2015 funding, PMI will provide full support in 26 districts and minimal

support in the 34 graduated districts. Based on the evaluation of 2014 operations, the number of structures to be sprayed may be adjusted. PMI will focus on providing technical assistance and support in-service training for trainer of trainers at federal and regional levels to increase the FMOH's and ORHB's capacity in planning and management of IRS operations, environmental compliance, and poison control. The exact allocations and specifications of insecticides will be determined upon completion and review of the 2014 IRS activities and the insecticide policy decision of the FMOH.

• **Entomological capacity building and monitoring ($500,000):** Resistance monitoring will be carried out in eight sites using WHO tube tests in different ecological zones of the country to continue documenting what is happening in the susceptibility/resistance status of the vector after change in the insecticide policy. Technical support will be provided to conduct CDC bottle bioassays (24 sites) and to coordinate entomological monitoring activities implemented by the FMOH in sites outside of Oromia. Behavioral outcomes will be monitored to detect any change in mosquito behavior, particularly outdoor biting changes, in response to the changes in the insecticide used for IRS. Insecticide residual life monitoring to obtain evidence for the selection of best alternative insecticide also continues to be a priority activity.

• **Entomological supplies and equipment ($10,000):** Provide critical supplies, reagents, and equipment for routine entomological monitoring activities and resistance and bionomic studies.

• **Entomological technical assistance ($36,300):** Provide three technical assistance visits from CDC/Atlanta for training, planning, and monitoring entomological activities given the expansion of entomological surveillance up to the national level.

• **Environmental compliance monitoring ($35,000):** Support for an external environmental compliance assessment of Ethiopia's IRS activities. Insecticide distribution, use, storage, and disposal as well as insecticide tracking systems and/or tools will be monitored.

MALARIA IN PREGNANCY (MIP)

NMCP/PMI Objectives

Ethiopia has a relatively low ANC coverage rate compared to other countries in the region. The 2011 DHS indicated that for Ethiopia as a whole, only 34% of mothers received antenatal care from a heath professional for their most recent birth in the five years preceding the survey, although this demonstrated an improvement from the 28% noted in the 2005 DHS. One woman in every five (19%) made four or more ANC visits during the course of her pregnancy, up from 12% in 2005. The median duration of pregnancy at the time of the first antenatal visit is 5.2 months. Furthermore, although pregnant women are at greater risk of severe disease from malaria, overall they have historically represented a small proportion (2 to 3%) of the total number of malaria outpatients and inpatients in Ethiopia according to annual HMIS surveillance reports. In that year within the IDSR, pregnant women accounted for 1.7% of all reported outpatients with malaria (14,864/1,104,157), 2.9% of reported malaria hospitalizations (574/20,130), and 1.7% of reported inpatient malaria deaths (10/585). Since that time, the IDSR was folded into the PHEM system, but specific MIP morbidity and mortality data were no longer published. In a study by Newman *et al.*, a cross-sectional survey of placental parasitemia at a stable (high) malaria transmission site in the sparsely populated Gambella Regional State noted 6.5% prevalence, whereas three other sites in unstable (i.e., low) transmission settings noted only 2.5% prevalence. Because of the relatively low prevalence of malaria infection during pregnancy, intermittent preventive treatment of pregnant women (IPTp) is not part of the Ethiopian National Malaria Prevention and Control Strategic Plan.

National Malaria Guidelines were updated in 2012 by the FMOH to include pregnancy issues; these are available by searching the website at http://www.moh.gov.et/web/pages/resources. Consistent with WHO guidance, these guidelines recommend oral quinine for uncomplicated *P. falciparum* malaria in the first trimester, and oral AL for the second and third trimesters. For uncomplicated mono-species *P. vivax* malaria, oral chloroquine is recommended in all trimesters. For severe malaria, pre-referral rectal artesunate and IV artesunate for inpatient treatment is recommended. Recent PMI supported in-vivo monitoring studies have documented that *P. vivax* infected persons in Ethiopia experience about three relapses within the next 12 months; such illness relapses could be especially harmful to pregnant and breastfeeding women unable to take primaquine, who have impaired immunity, an impaired nutritional status, and an increased risk of progression to severe or complicated malaria illnesses.

There is minimal if any LLIN distribution via ANC clinics, except through a small project that overlaps with PEPFAR. Distribution of LLINs via ANC is not part of the FMOH malaria control strategy. Approaches used by the FMOH to target pregnant women are to: (i) scale-up universal LLIN coverage and encourage pregnant women to use LLINs; and (ii) ensure availability of prompt diagnosis and treatment of clinical malaria cases during pregnancy at health facilities. The LLIN replacement scheme proposed in the NSP for Malaria Prevention and Control 2011-2014 and the new draft strategy (v. June 14, 2014) is the policy framework for continuous LLIN distribution primarily through the HEP. Nearly all LLINs are distributed by HEWs through mass campaigns every three years. Although the universal coverage strategy is to provide one LLIN per 1.8 persons, the HEW is guided by written instructions to make sure that pregnant mothers and children less than five years of age have preferential access to LLINs in these mass campaigns and educate communities to give priority to pregnant mothers and children, in case nets are not sufficient to cover the entire family. Increasing ANC coverage is also one of the FMOH's priorities, and is supported by USAID/Ethiopia MNCH, family planning, and reproductive health funding.

Progress During the Last 12 Months

In Ethiopia, only 34% of women had received antenatal care from a skilled provider and only 10% were attended by a skilled provider. The most important barrier to access to health services that women mentioned is availability of transport to a facility, followed by lack of money and distance to a health facility, according to the 2011 MIS. A major focus of ANC programs in Ethiopia is providing expanded access to quality healthcare through health centers and health posts, where PMI is supporting prompt access to diagnostic and treatment services for pregnant women. Furthermore, HEWs will play a key role in identifying and preferentially distributing LLINs to pregnant women in the communities.

PMI provided technical support to update the FMOH's malaria diagnosis and treatment guidelines that were published in early 2012. These guidelines were reinforced through trainings of HEWs through iCCM roll out that were completed by late 2013 that also discussed malaria prevention and case management in pregnancy. Social behavior change communication messages and training are being developed based on these guidelines. The updated NSP for malaria (2014-2020) was finalized, but implementation guidelines were still in development as of June 2014.

Few published data are available about the status of MIP in Ethiopia since the Integrated Disease Surveillance Reporting System (IDSR) surveillance data from mid-2008 to mid- 2009 were last published in the annual Health and Health- Related Indicators Report.

Plans and Justification

PMI continues to support the current FMOH policies that address pregnant women's special needs through malaria prevention and control, and improving prompt access to malaria diagnosis, and appropriate care and treatment services. Although IPTp itself is not part of the national strategic plan, with FY 2015 funding, PMI will support maternal and perinatal protection from malaria with Focused Antenatal Care (FANC) Services and Safe Motherhood and Adolescent Reproductive Health through an emphasis on anemia management and the prompt diagnosis and management of acute malaria in pregnant women. To implement these activities, PMI has leveraged the resources of other GHI activities, particularly those supported by PEPFAR and USAID/Ethiopia MNCH, family planning, and reproductive health funds, and will harmonize health care worker and midwifery training and education. This harmonization will focus on ensuring that health providers counsel mothers on early detection of anemia and illnesses with fever, the importance of iron and folate supplementation, as well as using a LLIN during pregnancy for the protection of the fetus. This activity will be closely coordinated with PMI support for case management strengthening and supportive supervision for health care workers at health centers and HEWs at health posts.

In the past, the IDSR system collected and reported pregnancy and species-specific malaria surveillance data, but published annual reports since 2009 have not been including these disaggregated data. There has been increased interest in Ethiopia concerning MIP from both the FMOH and Global Fund in recent months. The FMOH's updated NSP (2014-2020) mentions a plan to assess the burden of MIP in a stable transmission area and to explore the possibility of targeted IPTp activities in high risk regions. PMI encourages these efforts, and also proposes an additional Operational Research project (as explained below) that would provide additional insights into the malaria burden among pregnant women in Ethiopia including the relapse rate for *P. vivax* during pregnancy. PMI will continue to work with the FMOH to identify and review all available MIP surveillance data, and to encourage the future routine collection, analysis, and publication of disaggregated MIP data once again into the FMOH's annual surveillance reports. These enhanced surveillance and operational research efforts would aim to provide an appropriate evidence basis for any possible future health policy changes related to MIP in Ethiopia.

Proposed Activities with FY 2015 Funding ($500,000):

• **Expanding malaria in pregnancy services through safe motherhood and FANC ($500,000):** PMI will leverage resources from tuberculosis and PEPFAR to strengthen MNCH services. PMI will focus on pre-service education, especially on the three cadres identified as priority cadres by the GoE in the HSDP IV – midwives and nurse anesthetists – as well as HEWs. PMI will support training of HEWs and midwives to ensure pre- and in-service training to improve the case management of acute malaria in pregnant women.

• **Operational Research (OR): Pilot study of weekly chloroquine suppression for pregnant women with *P. vivax* after completing initial treatment with chloroquine to inform FMOH treatment guideline policy (see *Operational Research* section):** Primaquine therapy is contraindicated during pregnancy and during breastfeeding; thus women who have *P. vivax* infection during these times may experience excess morbidity and special risks due to frequent vivax relapses. PMI will support an operational research study to assess the feasibility of delivering chloroquine prophylaxis to pregnant women to inform the FMOH on appropriate treatment guidelines for improving the health of *P. vivax*-infected pregnant and breastfeeding women.

CASE MANAGEMENT

DIAGNOSIS

NMCP/PMI Objectives

In line with Ethiopia's long-standing policy that all patients with suspected malaria should receive a confirmatory diagnostic test before treatment is prescribed, PMI has supported scale-up of quality assured diagnostic testing at both health facility and community level since its launch in Ethiopia. The NSP 2014–2020 strategic objective for malaria diagnosis specifies that by 2017, 100% of suspected malaria cases are diagnosed using RDT or microscopy within 24 hours of fever onset. In achieving NSP targets of sustaining universal coverage of diagnosis at health centers, PMI has supported procurement of microscopes, laboratory supplies, and reagents, and is scaling-up quality assurance systems for malaria microscopy and RDTs. At the community level, support is being provided for procurement of RDTs and training and supervision of HEWs in iCCM of the sick child, including performance of RDTs for managing acute febrile illnesses.

Progress During the Last 12 Months

An analysis of micro-plan data indicates that Ethiopia has made significant progress in scaling-up diagnostic testing for malaria: the percentage of all malaria cases reported that were confirmed by RDT or microscopy increased from 83% in 2012 to 92% in 2013 (see Figure 6). Oromia has shown a significant achievement in reducing presumptive treatment of malaria from 99% in 2007 to 8% in 2013 (see Figure 7).

Figure 6. Proportion of malaria suspected cases tested with RDT or Microscopy in (a) 2011-2012 and (b) 2012-2013 (micro-plan data)

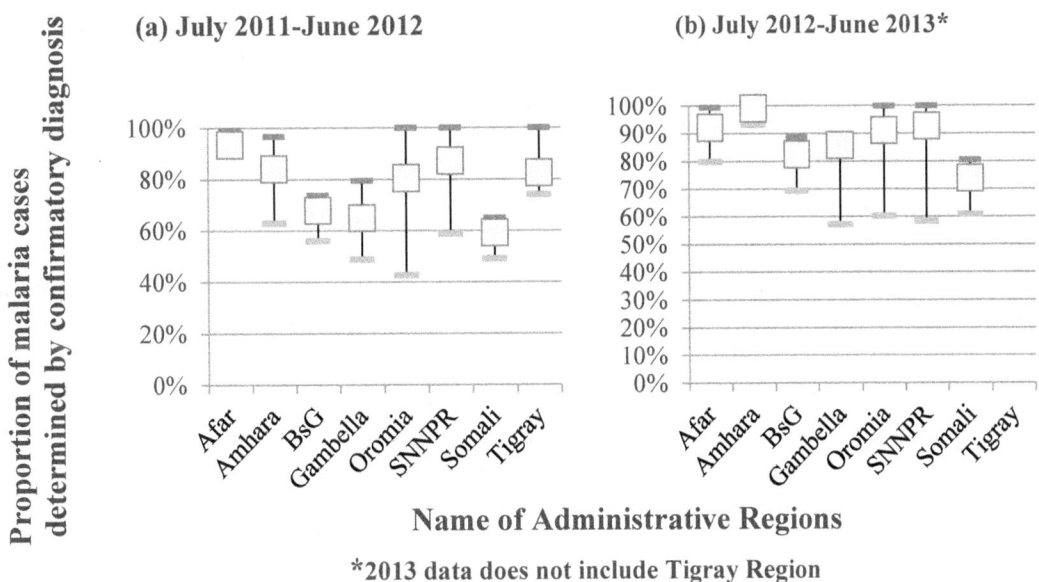

(a) July 2011-June 2012

(b) July 2012-June 2013*

Proportion of malaria cases determined by confirmatory diagnosis

Name of Administrative Regions

*2013 data does not include Tigray Region

Figure 7. Percentage of clinically treated malaria cases out of total cases in Oromia Regional State from 2006/07-2012/13

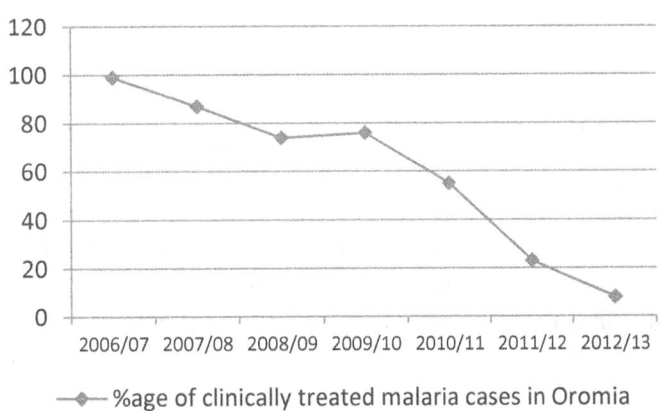

—◆— %age of clinically treated malaria cases in Oromia

In 2013, PMI procured and distributed 70 microscopes and microscopy kits for health centers. In addition, PMI-supported microscopy trainings are provided several times per year and are complemented by onsite supportive supervision and mentorship. PMI currently supports training and supervision of malaria diagnosis in 389 of the 700 health centers with laboratories in malarious areas in Oromia. PMI envisages scaling-up this support to all 700 facilities by 2016. Outside of Oromia Regional State, PMI also plans to provide enhanced facility-based supportive supervisions to 162, 94, 41, and 16 health centers in Amhara, SNNP, Tigray, and Dire Dawa Regional States, out of 784, 572, 165, and 17 facilities, respectively.

In order to reach more health facilities, PMI has built the capacity of EPHI to establish a national malaria slide archive, which will be used for training as well as panel testing. In addition, the capacity of seven regional laboratories was built in five additional regional states to conduct cascade training and supervision of peripheral laboratories. PMI also leverages resources from PEPFAR to integrate malaria laboratory strengthening in 72 health facilities that are currently supported by PEPFAR programs and supportive supervision of HEWs in over 1,500 health posts through other health programs. Furthermore, PMI has provided support to ORHB to deliver integrated supportive supervision for malaria, HIV, and tuberculosis to an additional 284 health facilities currently not supported by PMI.

In addition, PMI has supported the training of 260 laboratory personnel on an integrated malaria-HIV laboratory diagnosis and quality assurance/quality control (QA/QC) system. To date, PMI-supported QA/QC activities have largely been focused on microscopy in health centers, regional reference laboratories and hospitals. PMI has focused more on microscopy QA as the Global Fund has been primarily procuring RDTs for the past three years. The RDT QA/QC activities have been led by EHNRI, which also has the capacity to conduct lot quality testing. In addition, Ethiopia participated in a pilot assessment of dried tube specimens for assessing RDT sensitivity. While this has shown promising results, PMI is not currently pursuing this as we are awaiting a new generation RDT with embedded controls that will avoid the need for an external gold standard to assess RDT quality.

Furthermore, 26 laboratory supervisors have received training of trainers training from regional reference laboratories in Oromia, Amhara, Tigray, Dire Dawa, and SNNP Regional States. These supervisors are now planning to cascade basic trainings in all regional states of Ethiopia using funds from GoE and technical assistance from PMI. To improve the pre-service training of laboratory professionals and medical students on malaria diagnosis and treatment, training was provided to 31 university instructors from 8 major universities.

During the past 12 months, 246 health facilities were involved in an external QA scheme using blind rechecking. It has been recognized that there is insufficient human and financial resources to support blinded rechecking of blood slides for all health facilities at regional reference laboratories. Therefore, facilities that score greater than 90% slide reading agreement with the regional reference laboratory on three successive rounds of rechecking will be considered "graduated" so that additional facilities can then undergo rechecking. To date, 99 health facilities have graduated.

Progress has been made in expanding supportive supervision to more health facilities. Because of the large number of health facilities in Ethiopia, half of the facilities (389/700) in Oromia and a small number of facilities in other regions receive routine supervision for malaria diagnosis. PMI is exploring collaboration with PEPFAR to integrate supervision of malaria microscopy and RDTs into their supervision of laboratories in supported areas. In addition, PMI will work to assist regional states to strengthen sub-regional reference laboratories and support hospital laboratory staff to supervise nearby facilities that are not currently receiving supportive supervision.

Plans and Justification

PMI will build on the progress to date in scaling up diagnostic testing for malaria and accelerate expansion of quality assurance systems to cover more than 700 facilities in Oromia and other regional states. PMI will also expand training and support to all regional laboratories, to include Afar, Gambella, Harari, and Benishangul-Gumuz. PMI will further expand supervision to laboratories supported by PEPFAR by integrating malaria supervision modules into their supervision tools and by training their supervisors in malaria microscopy and performance of RDTs.

PMI will be building capacity for supportive supervision of malaria diagnosis in facilities currently being supported by EPHI, as well as in Regional Reference Laboratories. Building this capacity into existing supervisory activities will come at minimal additional cost and will help move Ethiopia towards scaling up national-level supervision activities to all facilities.

PMI will continue its support of clinical oversight of malaria diagnosis and case management activities of HEWs through an integrated supervision platform, and of clinicians at health centers through mentorship and supportive supervision. In addition, PMI will be supporting pre-service training of HEWs and clinicians in fever case management.

Table 10. RDT gap analysis, 2015-2017

	2015	2016	2017
Total number of suspected malaria fever cases	14,391,815	13,077,817	12,192,157
Country target for diagnostic coverage *(FMOH GF NFM Table 2 of June 14, 2014)*	100%	100%	100%
Diagnostic coverage by microscopy	30%	30%	30%
Diagnostic coverage by RDT	70%	70%	70%
Total number of RDTs to meet national need *(Per FMOH gap analysis, FMOH GF NFM Table 2 of June 14, 2014)*	**14,391,815**	**13,077,817**	**12,192,157**
PMI contribution	5,400,000	5,400,000	5,400,000
Available RDTs from GF and other sources	7,310,009	7,217,011	6,337,351
RDTs available (all sources)	**12,710,009**	**12,617,011**	**11,737,351**
Remaining RDT gap	**1,681,806**	**460,806**	**454,806**

The above number of suspected cases and RDT requirements come directly from the draft NSP (v. June 14, 2014) and Global Fund NFM concept note. The actual RDT requirements are likely to be much lower and adjustments will be needed as updated RDT gap numbers become available.

Proposed Activities with FY 2015 Funding ($5,550,000):

• **Procurement of RDTs ($3,800,000):** PMI will procure and distribute 5.4 million multi-species RDTs mostly to health posts. This will support the projected needs of the country.

• **Support for quality assurance system for microscopy and RDTs ($1,000,000):** Technical and programmatic support to health facility laboratories will be scaled up to more than 700 facilities in Oromia and other regional states and to more than 300 health centers in other regional states. Additionally operational support will be provided to all regional reference laboratories in Ethiopia as well as major regional hospitals. This will include support for refresher training, supervision, other QA/QC activities, and program monitoring. Training and accreditation will be provided to laboratory supervisors.

• **Procurement of laboratory equipment/supplies ($750,000):** PMI will build capacity of EPHI and regional reference laboratories to repair microscopes already in facilities. To promote standardization, PMI tries to ensure that malaria microscopes have similar formats and capabilities. In addition, PMI will support further procurement of approximately 230 microscopes and 230 laboratory kits to laboratories that conduct malaria microscopy in Oromia, Amhara, Tigray, and SNNPR.

• **Provide supportive supervision to HEWs (see *Treatment* section):** Continued support will be provided for integrated supervision of HEWs, which will include observation of management of patients.

TREATMENT

NMCP/PMI Objectives

One of the goals of the NSP for malaria 2014–2020 is to treat all confirmed malaria cases with appropriate antimalarial drugs and manage all severe cases according to the new treatment guideline. Current treatment policy recommends AL and chloroquine as the first-line drug for the treatment of uncomplicated *P. falciparum* and *P. vivax*, respectively. Mixed infections with *P. falciparum* are treated with AL. According to the new NSP, vivax malaria can be treated with primaquine if glucose-6-phosphate dehydrogenase (G6PD) status is known. For infants <5 kg of body weight and pregnant women in the first trimester, quinine should be administered. Rectal artesunate has been adopted as pre-referral treatment for severe malaria at the health post level. Intravenous or intramuscular artesunate (or IV/IM quinine, or IM artemether, if artesunate is not available) is recommended for treatment of severe cases at the health centers and hospitals. PMI has made a concerted effort to provide sufficient parenteral artesunate dosages, and support trainings of health care workers on how to use artesunate to completely replace parenteral quinine for severe malaria treatment in Ethiopia.

Progress During Last 12 Months

To date, PMI has procured over 8.9 million AL treatment doses for Ethiopia. As part of the national support, PMI has also procured over 7.88 million doses of chloroquine, 56,458 quinine doses, and 108,000 doses of rectal and 86,000 IV/IM artesunate. In addition, PMI has also supported the micro-planning of malaria commodities at the district level. This exercise has significant importance in allocation and distribution of malaria commodities based on malaria morbidity at the district level. Based on this micro-planning, annual ACT needs have decreased by 2 million doses relative to 2011/12, as a result of improved planning, decreased needs for contingency stocks, decreasing malaria burden, and increased utilization of diagnostic testing that has reduced the empirical treatment of patients with fever (see Figure 8).

Figure 8. Malaria case management commodity requirement trends, Ethiopia, 2011-2014

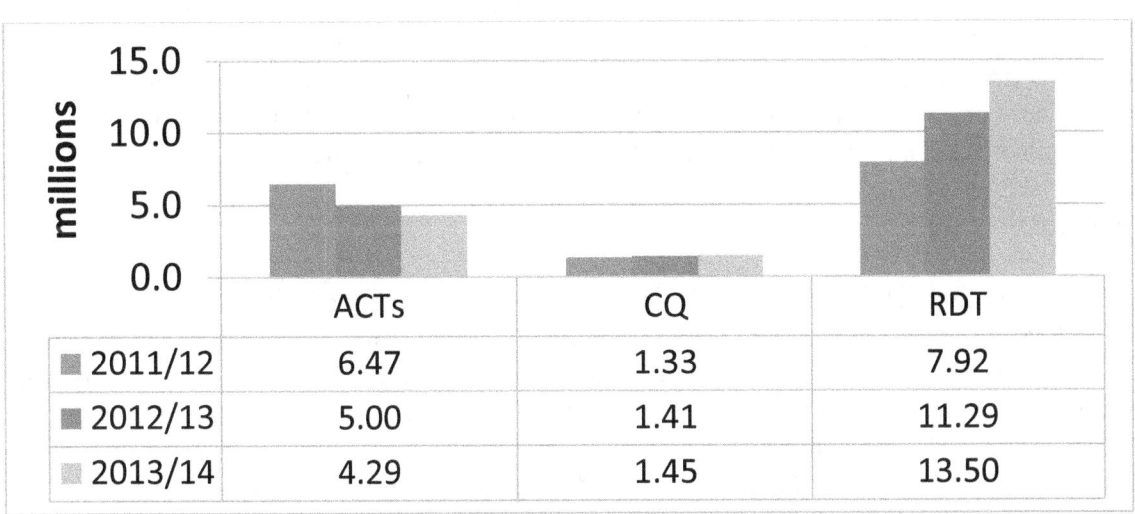

	ACTs	CQ	RDT
■ 2011/12	6.47	1.33	7.92
■ 2012/13	5.00	1.41	11.29
▨ 2013/14	4.29	1.45	13.50

Source: Micro-plan prior year morbidity data adjusted by15% for contingencies, and mal-distributions; RDT requirements are double the amount of reported prior year testing to ensure adequate testing capacity. ACTs are required for all presumed/ clinically treated cases, all mixed species infections, and all P. falciparum infections. Chloroquine quantifications for P. vivax cases adjusted by 15%.

PMI is working with ORHB, FMOH, and other implementing partners to support health worker training at both the health center and health post levels, including the roll-out of iCCM to community-level health posts in 301 districts in six regional states. In addition, 205 clinical personnel have been trained on appropriate fever case management. PMI will also support activities to improve performance standards and quality of the pre-service and in-service training; and support in-service training programs for 4,151 clinical officers and HEWs through the iCCM and Integrated Management of Neonatal and Childhood Illnesses Program.

PMI is supporting District Health Office staff in monitoring and supervision of health centers, and supports health center staff in their monitoring and supervision of health posts. This supervision is being integrated into established, USAID/Ethiopia-supported family planning/reproductive health and MNCH activities. The supervision is ensuring that case management is implemented effectively and in-line with FMOH guidelines. PMI, along with other partners, is assisting in reviewing the quality and competency of the supervisors, and helping to support refresher trainings and coaching to further improve supervisors' capacity. This includes providing training materials and checklists as well as transportation and other costs to ensure the supervision is actually taking place. During the past year, 309 health managers were trained on integrated supportive supervision in 301 *woredas*.

Ethiopia revised the malaria treatment guidelines in 2012. Major challenges in malaria treatment include clinicians' adherence to treatment guidelines, patients' adherence to treatment, and maintaining a continuous supply of effective medicines at the health post level and private facilities. Micro-planning data has shown improved surveillance and improved levels of laboratory confirmation. Although there appear to be enough ACTs imported into the country, there are uneven distributions to health facilities and there is an imperfect and poorly developed system for redistributing medicines between districts. Furthermore, ensuring adherence to malaria treatments has been challenging, especially in children.

The MIS 2011 survey suggests that about 29% of people initially receive care for febrile illnesses through the private sector. However, the capacity of the private sector to manage malaria well is limited, and they lack ACTs, RDTs, microscopy capacity, as well as rectal and IV artesunate. There is limited outreach or regulation from the FMOH to the private sector, and there is no platform to share national treatment guidelines or best practices.

Plans and Justification

With FY 2015 funding, PMI is procuring 2.6 million AL treatments for filling the existing gap (Table 11). PMI will also procure chloroquine, quinine, and rectal and IV artesunate as part of its national support (Table 12). Although Global Fund support is possible in the interim, it may be simpler for PMI and the FMOH if PMI's many partners' expertise in logistics and supply chains becomes more focused on the entirety of the supply chain and logistics issues as PFSA and other FMOH agencies try to build sustainable capacity to support the logistics of malaria case management.

Table 11. ACT gap analysis, 2015-2017

	2015	2016	2017
Total number of suspected malaria fever cases (FMOH NFM Annex 9)	14,391,816	13,077,817	12,198,157
Country target for diagnostic and treatment coverage (public sector)	100%	100%	100%
Total estimated cases of *P. falciparum (Per FMOH gap analysis, NFM Annex 9 includes confirmed and clinical cases, seasonal workers, epidemics)*	6,784,218	6,164,527	5,103,678
Number of ACT treatment doses needed (National, minimum) *(NFM 2014)*	**6,784,218**	**6,164,527**	**5,103,678**
Number of treatment doses needed for Oromia (PMI estimate from micro-plan)	934,345	934,345	934,345
ACTs available from PMI	2,600,000	2,600,000	2,600,000
ACTs available from GF and other sources (NFM Annex 9)	3,377,498	2,814,585	1,753,736
ACTs available (all sources)	**5,977,498**	**5,414,585**	**4,353,736**
Remaining ACT gap	**806,720**	**749,942**	**749,942**

Table 12. Chloroquine gap analysis, 2015-2017

	2015	2016	2017
Total *P. vivax* (Micro-plan 2012-2013)	1,258,131	1,258,131	1,258,131
Number of chloroquine treatments doses needed (National) *(micro-planning morbidity data adjusted by a factor of 15% for epidemics, under-reporting of negative cases and contingency)*	**1,258,131**	**1,258,131**	**1,258,131**
Number of chloroquine treatments doses needed (Oromia)	274,194	274,194	274,194
Chloroquine available from PMI	1,258,131	1,258,131	1,258,131
Chloroquine available from GF and other sources	0	0	0
Chloroquine available (all sources)	**1,258,131**	**1,258,131**	**1,258,131**
Remaining chloroquine gap	**0**	**0**	**0**

Proposed Activities with FY 2015 Funding ($5,102,400):

• **Procurement of ACTs for *P. falciparum*, chloroquine and primaquine for *P. vivax*, pre-referral treatments and drugs for severe malaria ($3,802,400):** PMI will support the procurement and distribution of 2.6 million AL treatments to meet the needs for Oromia based on the district-level micro-plan as well as a contingency amount for national-level distribution by the FMOH to fill gaps in other parts of the country. PMI will support the procurement and distribution of the entire estimated national need for chloroquine (i.e., 1.26 million treatments) and other antimalarial drugs, including drugs for severe disease and pre-referral care (i.e., rectal and parenteral artesunate) and primaquine. Chloroquine, pre-referral treatment, and drugs for severe malaria will be tested for quality at accredited laboratories following standardized protocol prior to shipment to Ethiopia.

• **Support for supervision and monitoring of HEWs in providing malaria treatment ($1,000,000):** Support to supervision and monitoring of malaria treatment at health centers and health posts in eastern Oromia, eastern Amhara, Dire Dawa, and Harari Regional States (which represent one-third of all of the HEWs in the country) will be continued. About 301 district health offices, 770 health centers, and more than 1,500 health posts will receive this supportive supervision. More than 300 health workers, including HEWs, will receive in-service training in reviewing new malaria case management guidelines, on-site supervision, and ensuring that case management reporting is complete and accurate.

• **Private sector support to case management ($300,000):** PMI will work with the regional health bureaus and 83 private health facilities in four regional states, including Oromia Regional State, to increase access to quality malaria services, including diagnostic testing and free antimalarial treatment to the clients in the private sector. This private-public partnership initiative project supported by PMI is one of the first attempts to understand private sector practices and challenges in Ethiopia, in order to improve case management of malaria.

• **Pre-service training of HEWs and clinicians in fever case management (no additional funding required):** PMI will support pre-service training of HEWs and midwives for integrated malaria case management. PMI will also ensure that malaria-specific updates for technical materials and guidelines are provided to USG-supported midwifery training and capacity building programs, including PEPFAR-funded activities focusing on the prevention of mother-to-child-transmission of HIV (PMTCT). In addition, capacity of 31 universities will be strengthened to provide quality training of ambulatory patient management. On-site mentoring will be provided for clinicians, nurses, and doctors in 100 selected health centers to improve malaria case management.

PHARMACEUTICAL MANAGEMENT

NMCP/PMI Objectives

The FMOH and PMI have been working to address multiple supply chain problems within all levels of the national drug management system, including malaria commodity bottlenecks, stockouts, and expiry. In 2005, the FMOH developed a Pharmaceutical Logistics Management Plan (PLMP) and later created the PFSA. Through mostly PEPFAR and Global Fund support, the FMOH radically redesigned the governance, policies, and infrastructure of the existing logistics system, establishing drug distribution "hubs" to directly supply health centers, health posts, and hospitals. Because of its complexity and cost, the new pharmacy supply chain system was slowly implemented and essential malaria commodities are still being largely distributed through other parallel donor-supported systems. Up until 2014, PMI has imported and distributed most of its malaria commodities (including ACTs) for Oromia Regional State through UNICEF per FMOH guidance, to be consistent with and complementary to Global Fund processes.

With PMI support, UNICEF has also conducted annual malaria commodity micro-planning activities to gather district-level data about malaria commodity inventories and estimated future malaria commodity requirements along with malaria morbidity reports. PMI has supported strengthening of PFSA by seconding staff. PFSA is currently providing pharmaceutical service for the public and private health institutions through eleven hubs situated in different regions of the country. In addition, PFSA will also be in charge of procuring and distributing equipment, medical supplies, contraceptives, vaccines, other family planning commodities, etc. The distribution will utilize a network of hubs/warehouses, with locations based on population density and operational feasibility. Currently, seven new hubs are under construction, intended to be operational by the end of 2014 in new regions i.e. Gambella, Benishangul Gumuz, Afar, and Somali. The agency strives towards ensuring sustainable supply chain system by implementing the Integrated Pharmaceuticals Logistics System (IPLS). The primary goal of the IPLS is to enable facilities to prepare bi-monthly commodity requests (orders) to the PFSA hub warehouse which supports them. The IPLS includes three separate but interrelated components: Health Commodity Management Information System (HCMIS) an automated information and inventory management tool for hospitals and selected health centers; a paper-based, manual IPLS version for the majority of health centers; and the health post resupply program which is the information procedures for resupplying health posts through health centers. In line with this change, PFSA designed and implemented both electronic and paper-based Logistic Management Information Systems at different levels in a phased approach. Logistic Management Information Systems is now being implemented in most of the regional hubs which started operations. As the capacities within PFSA improve and as PFSA assumes greater responsibility for pharmacy supply chains in Ethiopia, PMI will transition to distributing many and eventually all commodities through this system.

The Ethiopian FMHACA, a recently reorganized agency of FMOH, needs strengthening on many levels. It is responsible for regulating and registering medicines and ensuring the safety and quality monitoring of all medicines. It is also responsible for establishing and implementing quality assurance systems for the country, including post-marketing drug quality monitoring. PMI strengthens drug quality and safety monitoring capacities at FMHACA via post-marketing surveillance activities including use of Minilabs®. The Minilabs® are used to collect drug samples and provide preliminary field testing on quality of sampled medicines at customs check points, airports, and border ports of entry. Currently, there are seven sampling sites.

Progress During the Last 12 Months

PMI supported PFSA by embedding qualified personnel through funded partners within their facilities, and providing resources for the development of standard operating procedures and forms for the quantification, requisition, drug exchange/transfer, and management of malaria commodities. In addition, PMI has improved malaria commodity management in 190 public health facilities (114 in Oromia and 76 in other Regional States). These included health centers improved through training and supportive supervision. Malaria drug management data is now reported to the ORHB bi-monthly for 52 of these facilities in Oromia, including data on availability and expiry of antimalarial drugs, staff availability and capacity, and accurate reporting of antimalarial drug consumption. The data allows for monitoring and tracking of PMI- and ORHB-supported distribution of malaria commodities to health facilities.

In support of the FMHACA, PMI conducted a rapid assessment of Ethiopia's pharmaceutical QA system and established a post-marketing drug quality monitoring program in six locations in Ethiopia, including the establishment of drug testing Minilabs® and the training of GoE staff on drug sampling and testing. The fifth round of drug sampling and laboratory confirmatory testing was completed. The results of 2013 monitoring program indicate that all AL and most CQ sampled drugs have passed the drug quality control testing (see Table 13 below).

Table 13: Compendial test results of antimalarial drugs collected in 2013

Product	Total number of samples tested	Number of samples passed (%)
Artemether-Lumefantrine	34	34 (100)
Chloroquine phosphate	106	97 (91.5)
Quinine sulphate	20	18 (90)
Primaquine phosphate	5	1 (20)

In 2013, PMI expanded the post-market drug quality monitoring program to include regional FMHACA branch laboratories and further improved the regulatory capabilities of FMHACA. PMI also ensured that the activities are coordinated with other USG implementing partners and in-country stakeholders in a context of a changing PLMP and the nascent establishment of the PFSA. Additionally, through support from PMI and PEPFAR, the national reference laboratory under FMHACA achieved ISO-17025 accreditation, demonstrating a higher level of quality including employment of standard operating procedures and an overall laboratory quality system. ISO certification enables the laboratory to conduct various analytical pharmacopeial testing procedures for human drugs. PMI also supported relocation of the laboratory to a new site, which includes reinstallation and re-validation of all laboratory equipment.

With PMI support, micro-planning meetings with participants from all malaria-affected *woredas* and zones in Oromia were conducted annually since 2009, and in all regional states since 2011 to determine the requirements of ACTs, RDTs, and LLINs at the district level. The micro-plan is continuously being updated when distributions of commodities to the zones and districts occur. The updated micro-plan is being shared with PMI implementing partners to inform them when commodities will and should be available in the locations of implementation (e.g., health facilities). Partners then report back on an *ad hoc* basis to PMI on commodity availability within districts where they are already working, especially when focal stockouts or local epidemics are evident.

The ACT and RDT requirements were determined based on consumption records from previous years at health facilities and health posts of each *woreda*. The micro-plan considered the numbers of newly constructed health facilities and those expected to be operational in the following year. The results have subsequently been used to estimate the needs of pediatric and adult tablets of chloroquine to treat *P. vivax* malaria, and to prioritize and rationalize malaria commodity distributions through the year, based upon updated available inventory of supplies and epidemiological reports of increased local malaria activity (such as "hot-spot" districts). With FY 2015 funding, PMI will continue to support FMOH and all regional states in Ethiopia in this micro-planning process for malaria commodities that is now recognized as a best practice. In the near future, there is a plan to investigate opportunities of integrating micro-planning with PHEM, HMIS, and HCMIS, for improved data capturing for decision making in the malaria control program.

Micro-plans, while a very valuable annual activity, do not provide perfect estimates of resource and commodity requirements; specifically, these studies have not accounted for existing inventories or expiry dates of medicines or RDTs. Ultimately, in an epidemic-prone setting such as Ethiopia, redistribution of resources among or between districts may be needed to meet local needs that could not have been accurately forecasted from available data; such flexible redistribution plans or processes are typically not available. The PFSA does not yet appear to have the capacity to meet the dynamic demands of the malaria transmission season or to respond promptly to urgent malaria medication stockouts. Some malaria commodities cost substantially less when ordered six or more months in advance, and some commodities have expiry dates of only two years; these factors create additional costs and increase the risk of waste particularly when logistics systems have slow procurement and customs clearance processes, slow, infrequent, and inflexible delivery cycles, and are unable to redistribute resources in the periphery based upon current malaria caseloads that fluctuate locally from year to year and season to season.

The large geographical areas with many remote regions and seasonal rains cause major challenges to maintaining malaria commodity supply chains. PMI-funded pharmaceutical facility baseline assessment surveys and ongoing reports reveal continued supply chain problems for malaria drugs in all regional states. There continue to be focal shortages and stockouts of ACTs (especially pediatric doses) and chloroquine; expired drugs and near expiring RDTs; weak inventory control tools; inadequate medication records; and poorly organized and inadequate storage facilities.

Plans and Justification

The emerging capacities of PFSA and FMHACA provide an opportunity to take on more responsibility for pharmacy supply chains and antimalarial drug quality monitoring in the future, respectively. Strengthening pharmaceutical and malaria commodity supply chains will be a long term PMI investment. The micro-planning process has been recognized as a best practice in Ethiopia. Strengthening antimalarial drug management will also be needed throughout Ethiopia through a closer working relationship with PFSA. There will be an ongoing need to ensure quality of antimalarial drugs in Ethiopia to support quality malaria care and treatment in partnership with FMHACA.

Proposed Activities with FY 2014 Funding ($1,400,000):

• **Strengthening of antimalarial drug management ($750,000):** PMI will help sustain and expand the malaria drug management program from the current approximately 200 health centers covering approximately two-thirds of the malaria risk areas within Oromia, to support for strengthening health systems and pharmacy logistics for PFSA selected sites in all regional states of Ethiopia. The program will continue to focus on: Improving the management of malaria commodities, including quantification, forecasting, requisition, drug exchange/transfer, and expiry tracking/disposal;

- Improving the storage, organization, and security of drugs within health facilities and zonal/districts;
- Promoting the rational use of malaria drugs by training of PFSA and health facility level staff in drug management, as well as through on-site supervision; and
- Implementing the PMI end-use verification survey, ensuring that antimalarial drugs distributed with PMI funding are available at facilities and reach beneficiaries.

• **Strengthening PFSA pharmaceutical management capacities ($250,000):** PMI will provide support through a funded partner to PFSA to integrate malaria commodities in IPLS as well as to improve management of malaria commodities quantification, requisition, drug exchange/transfer, and expiry tracking/disposal. PFSA's capacity will also be built to procure, prepare, and distribute quality reagents such as Giemsa solution for malaria diagnosis.

• **Strengthening drug quality monitoring ($400,000):** PMI will continue to sustain and further improve the Ethiopia FMHACA's drug quality assurance program by:

- Supporting post-marketing drug quality monitoring in six sentinel sites in all regional states;
- Training staff of FMHACA central and five regional laboratories on quality control tests of antimalarials;
- Strengthening the GoE's central and regional quality control laboratories through training, technical assistance, sample collection, supportive supervision, and supply of equipment and reagents to FMHACA laboratories; and
- Improving data use and subsequent policy and regulatory measures.

• **Micro-planning surveys for estimating annual requirements and for assisting with distributions of malaria commodities (see *M&E* section):** With FY 2015 funding, PMI will continue to support FMOH through micro-planning meetings with participants from all malaria-affected *woredas* and zones in Ethiopia to determine the requirements of ACT treatments and RDTs and LLINs at the district level. PMI-supported micro-plan activities will be increasingly integrated with and harmonized with PFSA and FMOH's *woreda*-based planning activities in the future.

MONITORING AND EVALUATION

NMCP/PMI Objectives

Epidemic Detection and Response

Malaria epidemics in Ethiopia have been documented since the 1930s. A catastrophic malaria epidemic in 1958 was responsible for an estimated 3 million clinical cases of malaria and 150,000 malaria deaths. Since 1958, major epidemic years have occurred approximately every five to eight years (Tulu, A. N. "Malaria", In: Kloos, H. and Zein, A. Z., The Ecology of Health and Disease in Ethiopia, 1993, West View Press Boulder, San Francisco, Oxford, pp. 341-352). Guidelines for Malaria Epidemic Prevention and Control were updated in 2012 with support of PMI and are available on the FMOH's website. Updates about the current status of malaria outbreaks in Ethiopia were provided earlier in the Introduction, and the Malaria Situation chapters within the Strategy section. These new guidelines detail the human vulnerability factors, including population movement, as well as meteorological factors, such as rainfall, temperature, and humidity, that affect the occurrence of epidemics. The revised guidelines include setting detection thresholds at the health post level and strategies for mapping malaria micro-foci or micro-clusters.

Current methods for epidemic detection in Ethiopia rely on passive case detection of clinically diagnosed cases at health posts and health centers. In this system, the median weekly clinically diagnosed malaria cases over the previous five years are charted. Thresholds are set by either the third quartile (second highest number from the five previous years' data for that week) or double the previous year's number of cases in that week. If the number of cases in a given week exceeds the set threshold, the health worker is to report a potential epidemic. A rapid assessment team is then dispatched to confirm that an epidemic exists or is threatening, establish the cause and scale of the epidemic, and identify local capacity to respond. The guidelines recommend presumptive mass fever treatment with ACTs for fever cases if the test positivity rate is ≥50%. A stock of 15-20% of ACTs is to be held at the regional level for epidemic response. If there is potential for continued transmission, IRS will be implemented. For this reason, all districts with a potential for epidemics are advised to reserve a stock of insecticide for epidemic response and spraying operations would begin following either a three- or six-day training period for local spray operators.

In 2009, the PHEM surveillance system was developed to cover the entire country encompassing reporting from health posts, health centers, and hospitals. The PHEM aims to be a weekly multi-disease reporting system that collects a range of malaria indicators that are mostly related to outpatient malaria morbidity. The PHEM surveillance reporting covered 83% of districts throughout Ethiopia as of 2013, aiming to provide weekly reports from all health facilities, including health posts, through district health offices. Functionally, though, most districts only provide monthly reports, and rural health post reporting has lagged behind most other facilities. The PHEM depends on accurate and timely information being reported from HEWs and health facilities, so building that capacity though the health post level is essential. Malaria cases are reported by two age groups (less than five and more than five years of age) including clinical malaria (outpatient and inpatient), confirmed malaria by species. Assuming that improved IRS coverage and LLIN use will continue to reduce malaria transmission, the focus of malaria control and elimination will increasingly turn towards enhancing surveillance with the aim of halting ongoing transmission, and to investigate local vs. imported cases, and to prevent re-establishment of focal transmission in previously malaria-free areas.

Monitoring & Evaluation

With PMI support, a National Malaria M&E Plan was developed in 2011. This plan aimed to coordinate the collection, analysis, and management of malaria data to inform programmatic decisions and to assess whether the goals of the NSP for Malaria Prevention and Control 2011 – 2015 (*see Strategy section*) are being achieved. Additional discussions and adaptations of PMI's M&E activities are needed to support the new draft NSP for malaria for 2014-2020, and the FMOH's Global Fund Concept Note (draft June 7, 2014).

Currently, Ethiopia has a paper-based system of data collection at the health facility level; how-ever, these data have not always been optimally analyzed or used for decision-making and resource allocation at the local, regional, or national level. Consequently, Ethiopia's FMOH is in the process of revising the HMIS, while making some reporting electronic. This revised HMIS, which includes a total of 106 indicators and is primarily supported via funds from PEPFAR and the Global Alliance for Vaccines and Immunization, aims to provide one standardized set of health indicators nationally. Unfortunately, HMIS reports quarterly from health centers and hospitals at district level (no data reporting from health post) and reports of these data are not published for one or two years after they are collected. The most relevant and accurate data contained in these reports are inpatient cases and malaria deaths, although over 83% of health facilities are reporting on outpatients cases as of 2013. There are only two malaria-specific indicators in the HMIS:

- Malaria cases reported per 1,000 population, disaggregated into clinical and confirmed cases, with the latter further disaggregated by species, i.e., *P. falciparum*/other, among:
  - children under five years of age, and
  - people at least five years of age; and
- Malaria case fatality rate among:
  - children under five years of age [inpatients]
  - people at least 5 years of age [inpatients]

PHEM was designed to detect outbreaks for 20 priority events that cause public health emergencies, one of which includes malaria. PMI supports the PHEM system, which aims for weekly malaria morbidity reports from hospitals, health centers and also rural health posts. PMI's support is targeted to enhance reporting from rural health posts where half of all malaria morbidity is detected and treated, and to enable reporting of more complete RBM-MERG indicators on a weekly basis. As with previous PMI-supported malaria surveillance sentinel sites, PMI support could include data collection, analysis, training and supervisory visits.

PHEM and HMIS report to different directorates within FMOH, have separate staffing and reporting structures, and serve different functions. There are no plans to integrate these at this time. Reporting completeness has rapidly improved for both PHEM and HMIS. PHEM reporting completeness is now 83%, and HMIS completeness is 85-95%. The reported PHEM malaria totals will be nearly double compared to HMIS since it includes data from health posts which manages approximately half of the cases. The inpatient malaria totals should be about the same.

Field Epidemiology and Laboratory Training Program: Ethiopia began its FELTP in October 2008 with technical assistance from CDC as a two year, full-time, postgraduate competency-based training program consisting of about 25% class work and 75% field residency. Trainees are closely supervised and provide epidemiologic service to the FMOH. Graduates of FELTP will receive a Master's Degree in Public Health and Field Epidemiology. The program will join the African Field Epidemiology Network and work through the Ethiopian Public Health Association and EHNRI.

Progress during the Last 12 Months

The malaria module was removed from the Ethiopia DHS 2011 and an MIS survey was conducted in the same year separately due to a variety of technical and practical reasons. In particular, because of the focal nature of malaria in Ethiopia related to altitude strata, the sampling frame for a malaria survey is quite different from that of a general health survey. The sampling frame for the MIS focuses solely on areas with malaria risk (i.e., <2,500 meters elevation). In addition, because of the highly seasonal nature of malaria transmission in Ethiopia, it has not been optimal to include malaria into the DHS, which have been conducted in the dry season.

Results from a recently completed OR study that assessed seroprevalence in schools showed a wider prevalence range than microscopy for both *P. falciparum* (0-50% *vs* 0-12.7%) and *P. vivax* (0-53.7% and 0-4.5%), respectively. Overall, 11.6% (688/5,913) were *P. falciparum* seropositive and 11.1% (735/6,609) *P. vivax* seropositive; compared to 1.0% and 0.5% microscopy positive, respectively. PMI is supporting an OR study to assess the utility of conducting serologic testing using previously collected dried blood spots from the 2011 MIS to provide information to guide PMI on collection of biomarkers in household surveys in settings where malaria transmission is very low and/or seasonal. A service provision assessment (SPA) survey is underway in 2014, but results are not expected until sometime in late 2015.

Table 14. Monitoring and evaluation activity 2007-2016

Data Source	Survey Activities	Year									
		2007	2008	2009	2010	2011	2012	2013	2014	2015	2016
Household surveys	Demographic Health Survey (DHS)*					X					X
	Malaria Indicator Survey	X				X				X	
	EPI survey*						X				
Health Facility and Other Surveys	School-based malaria survey					X		X			
	Hospital Survey*	X				X					
	Oromia Health Facility survey						X				
	SPA survey*								X		
Malaria Surveillance and routine system support	Maintenance of Epidemic Detection Sites					X	X	X	X	X	
	National malaria commodities micro-plan					X	X	X	X	X	X
	HMIS*	X	X	X	X	X	X	X	X	X	X
	PHEM*	X	X	X	X	X	X	X	X	X	X
Therapeutic	*In vivo* efficacy testing			X		X*		X		X	X
Entomology	Entomological surveillance and resistance monitoring					X	X	X	X	X	X
Other Data Sources	Malaria Impact Evaluation								X		

*Not PMI-funded

Epidemic Detection and Response

PMI is providing support for the development of a strengthened Epidemic Surveillance and Response system in Oromia at the community, district, zonal, and regional levels. In order to detect epidemics quickly, PMI has started supporting strengthening of the alert system and health worker trainings for early epidemic detection. Many districts have inadequate epidemic preparedness plans and lack sufficient contingency funds to respond. Lack of skilled health personnel and poor coordination and management compound the problem. Although District Health Offices and Zonal Health Bureaus are instructed by national guidelines to have a 10-15% stockpile of malaria commodities, this is often not feasible due to planning and funding restrictions or increased clinical demand for these supplies. The ability to detect and respond to epidemics is also restricted by the existing HMIS, which is based upon reporting from only health centers and hospitals on a quarterly basis. While the PHEM system that aims for weekly malaria reporting is rapidly improving, prolonged delays in reporting are still common. Better tools including detailed risk maps are needed to improve targeting of malaria resources.

Malaria risk maps: Given the varying epidemiologic profile of Ethiopia, resource allocation for malaria prevention and control activities must be targeted strategically. Malaria risk mapping is critical to improve targeting PMI and other program resources, and to track progress at the community level. PMI supported the development of a detailed malaria risk map in Oromia, identifying areas at risk for malaria, including epidemic-prone areas, based on data available from cross-sectional school-based surveys. Due to the low malaria prevalence only a crude risk map could be developed so far. It is expected that further analysis of samples using serology as well as analysis of prospective health facility data will ensure the development of a risk map with greater resolution. Of note, EPHI has established serology testing capacity at the national level. They are currently testing the samples collected from the school-based survey. Preliminary results show that microscopy prevalence ranged from 0-12%, but serologic prevalence provided more variability from 0-60%. Several sites with 0% microscopy prevalence had higher serologic prevalence and furthermore, sites with serology prevalence of 0% provide invaluable information about longer malaria exposure. Results are expected to be available from these studies by late 2014. In addition, WHO has been developing a nationwide risk map based on incidence and climate data. The FMOH produced a draft NSP (version June 7, 2014) that included a risk mapping scheme based upon API that was presented earlier.

Malaria Indicator Survey: PMI supported the 2011 MIS, which assessed coverage, access, and use of malaria interventions. The final report is currently available on the FMOH website (see *Indicators* section). PMI not only financially supported this activity, but also provided significant technical assistance in all areas including all data collection and analytic support. The results showed a continued low prevalence of malaria by microscopy at 1.3% below 2,000 meters, with very low (0.1%) prevalence above 2,000 meters altitude.

The FMOH and EPHI are in the midst of planning for another similar MIS survey involving many partners including PMI with field work scheduled for late 2015.

Malaria Impact Evaluation: PMI is completing a comprehensive evaluation to determine the impact of malaria control interventions since 2000 on malaria mortality and morbidity in Ethiopia. This analysis considered all available data and contributions from all donors and the FMOH. Results of the impact evaluation were discussed earlier in the Coverage and Impact Indicators section. A final comprehensive report from this impact evaluation is expected in late 2014, and a RBM Progress and Impact Series report may be published in 2015.

Malaria Commodities Micro-plans: PMI supported annual micro-planning meetings with participants from all malaria-affected *woredas* and zones in Oromia since 2009 and for all of Ethiopia since 2011 to determine the requirements of RDTs, ACTs, and LLINs at district level. In addition to the commodity quantification, micro-planning also gathers district level data on malaria cases on an annual basis, which serves as an audit to assess completeness of malaria reporting of the routine surveillance system. This triangulation has been very useful in the PMI impact evaluation and other details are mentioned in the MOP background and epidemic sections. The micro-plan is being updated annually when commodities are distributed to the zones and districts. As mentioned elsewhere, it is expected that the micro-planning process will be increasingly integrated and harmonized with PFSA and with FMOH's *woreda*-based forecasting processes in the future.

Field Epidemiology and Laboratory Training Program: In 2011, three Ethiopian FELTP residents supported a comprehensive evaluation of PMI's ten epidemic detection sites. In late 2012, three FELTP residents participated (along with a CDC Epidemic Intelligence Service (EIS) Officer) in a *P. vivax* therapeutic efficacy trial with chloroquine versus AL with or without primaquine after G6PD testing. Another FELTP resident has nearly completed a project that investigates the feasibility of using dried tube specimens of standard concentrations of previously laboratory-cultured *P. falciparum* as a reagent to assess the quality of malaria RDTs and the performance of health care workers in performing RDTs in field conditions (oral presentation at the ASTMH 2013 meeting). Another resident presented data at the Atlanta CDC EIS conference in 2014 concerning a cluster of 10,000 acute febrile illnesses in an Ethiopia city that all tested negative by malaria laboratory tests, but was determined to be the first documented dengue fever outbreak in Ethiopia. Several other FELTP residents are finalizing protocols to investigate the epidemiology of malaria in various parts of Ethiopia or to evaluate malaria intervention coverage.

Plans and Justification

PMI will continue to provide technical assistance in improving the overall surveillance systems, which includes the HMIS and the PHEM. However, as these systems are not yet fully functional, PMI will continue to enhance these capabilities and support the select sentinel sites in Oromia to collect comprehensive, real-time malaria data and if necessary, provide technical assistance for establishing additional enhanced malaria surveillance sites where resistance to antimalarial medications and insecticides will also be monitored. Furthermore, PMI will continue to conduct annual national malaria commodities micro-planning. PMI will continue to support nationally representative household surveys to obtain key PMI coverage outcome indicators periodically and explore other diagnostic tools, for example, serology to monitor progress in Ethiopia.

Proposed Activities with FY 2015 Funding ($1,512,100):

• **Antimalarial drug therapeutic efficacy study ($110,000):** PMI will support ongoing periodic assessments of the effectiveness of currently used antimalarial drugs, in order to detect and mitigate possible introduction or emergence of drug resistance that could cause harm to patients with malaria illness in Ethiopia, and reduce PMI program impact. K13 resistance marker monitoring will be incorporated in the standard WHO *in vivo* protocols for all treatment failures and a proportion of the cured. PMI will support standardized sample collection and analysis.

• **LLIN durability study ($100,000):** An assessment will be made of LLIN durability at set intervals post distribution, to determine if policies that assume LLINs are still effective for three years are valid in the Ethiopian context.

• **Strengthening the PHEM system and epidemic response ($500,000):** Through PEPFAR funding, the GoE has established enhanced health management information systems in 143 malaria hotspot districts at the health center level in the country. With FY 2015 funding, PMI will strengthen reporting of malaria cases from the health post to the health centers in these districts to strengthen malaria epidemic detection and response which is not captured in the current system. The lessons learned from the Epidemic Surveillance and Response SMS system will inform this activity.

• **Strengthening epidemic surveillance and response ($200,000):** PMI will continue to strengthen the capacity of community-level HEWs and HEW supervisors to detect and respond to increases in malaria caseloads or epidemic outbreaks at the community level and HEW supervisor training, integrated supervisions, and regular field visits in 293 districts in six regional states (approximately one-third of the country). The purpose of the activity is to strengthen surveillance in the health care delivery system as a whole, leveraging the project's reach and ability to communicate with regards to occurring epidemic outbreaks, thereby ensuring a timely response. When outbreaks are detected at community level, PMI will follow up to ensure that ORHB, FMOH, and EPHI are notified, so that a coordinated response can be implemented. If new approaches to improve epidemic surveillance are found to be effective (e.g., mapping of malaria micro-clusters; school-based surveillance), this project platform will be used to scale up these approaches to national level.

• **Strengthening data management capacity ($100,000):** The FMOH has various systems for obtaining health data ranging from HMIS, PHEM system reports, and other fiscal, laboratory and supply chain reports. There are gaps in capacity to analyze data and reports, and to complete requests for additional funding from various malaria donors. PMI will support the FMOH to address these data management capacity gaps.

• **National malaria commodities micro-plan ($340,000):** PMI will support an annual assessment of malaria commodity gaps from the perspective of district malaria control officers who also report annual malaria morbidity.

• **M&E CDC TDY ($12,100):** One TDY visit to provide technical assistance for surveillance, M&E activities, and/or operational research studies.

• **FELTP ($150,000):** The GoE has requested that the FELTP expand to accommodate 23 trainees annually. Substantial malaria projects involving FELTP residents began in 2011 in Ethiopia. PMI will continue to support at least three trainees who will focus their field training on malaria prevention and control, including malaria outbreak detection and response activities, and an evaluation of malaria surveillance efforts.

OPERATIONS RESEARCH

NMCP/PMI Objectives:

There is clearly an ongoing and routine need by malaria programs to monitor and evaluate issues related to effectiveness of heavily funded program interventions including vector insecticide resistance (discussed previously in the Prevention/IRS section) and whether malaria case management policies and guidelines are optimal. Drug resistance monitoring and LLIN durability studies should also occur regularly in each country per WHO and/or PMI guidelines, as was previously mentioned in the M&E section. Additional *ad hoc* operational research projects are needed when routine monitoring and evaluation systems are insufficient, such as when there are few data to inform policy and guideline changes that may or may not be needed, or when proposed policy changes would affect relatively few people.

***P. vivax* Malaria in Pregnancy:** Recent PMI supported *P. vivax* research has documented that persons with acute illness from *P. vivax* may experience as many as three relapses per year when living in malaria endemic areas despite currently recommended chloroquine treatment. While *P. vivax* infections are clearly harmful to the pregnant woman and child, primaquine radical cure is contraindicated in pregnant and breastfeeding women, thus placing both of these at risk of *P. vivax* relapse. Chloroquine has long been used to prevent *P. vivax* infections in malaria endemic areas, but chloroquine use to suppress clinical infections and relapses after initial *P. vivax* illness has not been well studied in Ethiopia. It is expected that the FMOH will require results of a targeted OR studies to assess the feasibility/adherence to inform possible considerations for a policy change to permit or encourage weekly chloroquine prophylaxis for pregnant women and breastfeeding women until primaquine radical cure can be safely administered.

Assessment of Primaquine (Single Dose) for Falciparum Transmission Interruption: Although single dose primaquine has been recommended by WHO to reduce falciparum malaria transmission in elimination settings and in areas of artemisinin resistance, there is little data to support the effectiveness of this intervention on transmission. With the NSP including single, low-dose primaquine for treatment of falciparum cases, there is an opportunity to systematically assess the effectiveness and possible excess adverse events of this policy change as it is implemented in the proposed 50 elimination districts.

Progress During the Last 12 Months

School-Based Surveillance: Ashton *et al.* performed school-based surveillance in Oromia Regional State involving blood smears from 20,899 children from 197 schools (*Malar J* 2011 Feb 3;10(1):25). There were 0.56% of the children who had malaria parasites detected, with prevalence at schools ranging from 0 to 14.5%, and a suggestion of clustering. School seroprevalence showed a wider prevalence range than microscopy for both *P. falciparum* (0-50% vs. 0-12.7%) and *P. vivax* (0-53.7% vs. 0-4.5%), respectively. Ashton *et al.* conducted a similar school-based surveillance project in SNNPR Region in 2012, with data analysis mostly completed and initially reported to the FMOH by late 2013. Initially, 104 (2%) of 5,145 surveyed school-aged children had malaria parasites detected by RDT screening; girls had a lower (but not significant) odds of infection compared to boys (OR=0.60, 95% CI 0.31-1.18, p=0.137). No malaria epidemics were noted at any of the 20 schools studied in phase 2 of this project. Only about one-third of school absentees were attributable to any illnesses, and the more common reasons for school absences was to assist with farming or domestic chores. About ten percent of children cumulatively appeared to "drop out" permanently as the semester progressed. The estimated cost of scaled-up malaria school-based surveillance was $5,438 per district per year, assuming 18 schools per district.

Serologic Assessment to Monitor Malaria Burden: Repeated MIS have noted malaria prevalence by microscopy around 1%. In the low transmission and highly seasonal, epidemic-prone context of Ethiopia, serology as a measure of period prevalence might provide a more useful measure to monitor malaria progress. Serologic testing capacity had been established at EPHI and refresher training by the London School of Hygiene and Tropical Medicine has been conducted. Following procurement of all necessary reagents, EPHI aims to complete testing of all already collected MIS samples in 3-4 months. In addition to the antigens previously tested in the school-based survey, additional antigens will be tested on a multiplex platform by CDC with CDC funding to assess a broader range of potential antigens.

Assessment of G6PD Deficiency: Although Ethiopia is noted to have low G6PD prevalence, no recent or genotypic data exist for Ethiopia to inform the risks of implementing primaquine therapy for either *P. falciparum* or *P. vivax* case management. Using the same dried blood spots collected during the MIS, a random sample are being tested by PCR-RFLP for A- and Mediterranean variants. A scientist from EPHI received training from a CDC Malaria Branch laboratory to learn these techniques in early 2014. Over 200 samples have been tested in Atlanta and the remaining samples will be completed in EPHI laboratories. The results of this study will influence FMOH policy and clinical guidelines regarding PQ use, both for multi-dose radical cure of vivax and for single dose use in falciparum malaria. If a low prevalence of major deficiencies is identified, as is suspected, we believe the FMOH will consider modifying treatment guidelines to include primaquine therapy without prior G6PD testing.

Table 15. Operational Research

Completed OR Studies			
Title	**Start date**	**End date**	**Budget**
School-based surveillance	Oct 2011	Sept 2013	$200,000
Ongoing OR Studies			
Serologic assessment to monitor malaria burden	March 2014	Oct 2015	$70,000
Assessment of G6PD variant prevalence	Jan 2014	Jan 2015	$90,000
Planned OR Studies FY 2015			
Pilot study of chloroquine prophylaxis for pregnant women diagnosed with *P. vivax* malaria	Spring 2016	Spring 2017	$150,000
Evaluation of single-dose primaquine roll out on falciparum transmission	Fall 2015	Fall 2017	$500,000

Proposed Activities with FY 2015 Funding ($674,200):

- **Pilot study of chloroquine prophylaxis for pregnant women diagnosed with *P. vivax* malaria ($150,000):** This OR study will prospectively study the feasibility and effectiveness of weekly chloroquine on *P. vivax* relapses after initial clinical malaria illness among pregnant and breastfeeding women, until primaquine therapy can safely provide a radical cure. Although adherence is likely to be higher in a study setting and also when limited to women with a diagnosis of vivax malaria, adherence as a key factor in effectiveness will be assessed.

- **Evaluation of single-dose primaquine roll out ($500,000):** This study will systematically monitor the effects of primaquine roll out on malaria transmission and reported drug toxicity and health costs through careful review of routinely collected malaria incidence data and cross sectional surveys to assess parasite burden and multiplicity of infection. The FMOH's decision to implement single-dose primaquine without G6PD testing in their elimination districts will likely await the results of the G6PD genotyping study assessing the prevalence of A- and Med variants in Ethiopia. If the FMOH pursues addition of primaquine in falciparum case management on a wider scale, then the clinical guidelines would need to be updated appropriately to ensure adequate pharmacovigilance e.g. monitoring urine color changes.

- **Operational research CDC TDYs (24,200):** Two TDY visits to provide technical assistance for Malaria OR studies.

SOCIAL AND BEHAVIOR CHANGE COMMUNICATION

NMCP/PMI Objectives

According the NSP for 2014–2020, the SBCC objective states: "By 2020, all households living in malaria endemic areas will have the knowledge, attitudes and practices towards malaria prevention and control." In achieving this objective, the NSP focused on utilization of HEWs, with the support of HDAs and model family households. Despite the absence of a malaria-specific communication strategy, the national health communication strategy launched in 2004 provides a guide for all areas of health including malaria prevention and control. This strategic document is currently under revision and will give details of malaria communication approaches and implementation at various levels.

According to the new NSP, the strategies for community empowerment and mobilization include:

- conducting integrated refresher training on malaria SBCC for HEWs
- developing and integrating the malaria communication strategy into the national communication strategy
- increasing the use of supportive mass media
- integration of malaria prevention and control into school programmes
- conducting advocacy to gain strong commitment of the local leaders in malaria elimination districts
- production and distribution of IEC/behavior change communication (BCC) materials
- conducting orientation workshop for HDAs on community mobilization including iCCM service and its importance
- conducting formative research on knowledge, attitudes, and practices

The Ethiopian DHS 2011 shows the level of exposure to mass media is low in Ethiopia. Only 22 % of women and 38% of men listen to the radio at least once a week. In addition, 68% of women aged 15–49 and 54% of men in the same age group did not have access to any of the three common media types (TV, radio, or print). Nationally, progress has been observed in terms of net use among children under five in households that owned nets. According to the MIS, the percentage of children under five who had slept under a mosquito net the night preceding the survey was 60% in 2007, increasing to 65% in 2011. Tigray Region demonstrated the highest increase, with 47% in 2007 and 68% in 2011. Oromia Region showed a decrease in net use by children under five to 55%. National findings showed no improvement in net use among pregnant women in 2011 compared to 2007. SNNP Region demonstrated the highest improvement in net use among pregnant women from 63% in 2007 to 75% in 2011.

The SBCC's role in achieving NMCP objectives in malaria control across interventions is clearly stated in the NSP. This includes carrying out intensive SBCC to improve health care seeking behaviour for diagnosis and adherence to treatment, and demand creation to increase ownership, utilization, and care and repair of LLINs. It is also highlighted that the FMOH, in collaboration with partners (including the private sector), will support general promotion of LLINs. Furthermore, the BCC activities also include community involvement for IRS acceptance and larval control activities including larviciding and environmental management.

Currently, there is a well functioning malaria-specific communication technical working group consisting of technical experts from FMOH's health education and communication team, malaria case team, and malaria partners. The working group provided technical guidance and assistance during the development of the NSP and will continue to support the Ministry in coordination and designing of malaria-specific communication guidelines, tools, and materials.

Progress During the Last 12 Months

Since 2009, PMI has provided assistance to the FMOH to carry out malaria BCC activities. Working with the regional, zonal, and district offices as well as HEP including HDAs, PMI has delivered critical SBCC activities. The C-Change project over its five years of operation has provided support to the FMOH by bringing a mix of skills, experience, and creativity to design and implement high impact malaria communication strategies. The project's work involved the use of mass media, interpersonal communication, community engagement, and participatory training to empower Ethiopian families to undertake malaria prevention and control activities. The end-line evaluation for this project revealed that there were a lot of positive changes compared to the baseline survey in the project areas. At the end of the project the percentage of households providing priority to children under five years of age to sleep under nets rose from 38% to 75% while the percentage of pregnant mothers having slept under a net the previous night rose from 21% to 54% in the households that owned at least one net. This program has also strengthened the regional, *woreda*, and *kebele* capacities in establishing and sustaining a culture for LLIN use. This effort was also complemented by hang-up campaigns in collaboration with the US military especially targeting the most vulnerable groups, i.e., pregnant women and children under five. Increasing community awareness about the effectiveness of IRS, improving treatment-seeking behavior for malaria (e.g., timeliness, appropriateness) and increasing community knowledge regarding malaria diagnosis, treatment, prevention, and control were also among the major activities of this program.

During 2014, PMI/Ethiopia initiated and supported two local organization's community based malaria BCC activities, as part of the USAID/Ethiopia Local Capacity Development program. These community-based malaria SBCC activities are being implemented in selected zones of Oromia and Amhara Regions for a three-year period (2014-2016). In Oromia Region, during the first half of 2014, start-up activities such as baseline assessments, community sensitization and training on malaria BCC were carried out. These project activities were intended to complement and support the national malaria SBCC activities through capacity building of selected schools and faith-based organizations (FBO) in high malaria transmission areas for conducting malaria SBCC activities at community level in coordination with HEP. The project uses harmonized malaria messages (eight essential malaria actions and four do-able actions) derived from previous PMI-supported SBCC projects and conducts SBCC-related activities in coordination with HEWs. This includes:

- conducting participatory baseline assessments
- providing trainings in 18 primary and secondary schools for teachers and antimalarial club students, 13 religious places and community leaders, parents and families
- supporting schools, mosques and churches on malaria communication promoting increased and consistent utilization of LLINs
- Increased health care seeking for malaria diagnosis and treatment and increased acceptance of IRS spraying and vector control activities

Specific to the Amhara Region SBCC project, 25 primary schools in 24 *kebeles* were identified for the first year project activities and so far 25 school malaria clubs were established and 105 individuals including participants from different sector offices (education, agriculture, women and children offices) participated in community sensitization workshops. In addition, during this period 625 peer education manuals were distributed to 15 schools, training of trainers programs on malaria SBCC were provided to 146 individuals including school teachers, HEWs, FBO leaders and communication workers. A baseline survey on malaria knowledge, attitudes, and practices has been conducted in collaboration with WHO's regional office and Bahir Dar University. Moreover, the project hosted an experience sharing visit to PMI's community-based malaria SBCC activities during the celebration of the 2014 World Malaria Day. Similarly, in Jimma Zone, project start-up activities have been carried out in 45 *kebeles* in three districts and close to 100 out of 181 individuals from 50 schools and 33 FBOs have already received malaria communication training.

Plans and Justification

With FY 2015 funding, malaria SBCC activities will be more integrated and coordinated with other health BCC activities for PMTCT, tuberculosis, family planning/reproductive health, MNCH, and nutrition. PMI will also continue to support local organizations through an Annual Program Statement mechanism to build local capacity in malaria key message communications.

Social behavior change communication partners will provide capacity building and coordination support to the Health Education Team at the FMOH and will review and harmonize the existing malaria SBCC tools and materials to deliver them through appropriate media channels based on evidence. Interpersonal communication such as entertainment education, using schools, and religious institutions will be encouraged. Promotional efforts on consistent and proper ITN use will be scaled up and will use alternative SBCC interventions to reach target groups with no access to radio and television. Suggested interventions include school programs and community meetings as well as other creative methods. Focus will be put on strategies initiated by the communities themselves, i.e., through HDAs. PMI's community-based SBCC activities will complement and reinforce the government's community-based health communication efforts by mobilizing school and faith-based communities as change agents.

Social behavior change communication activities through mass media and rural communications campaigns, supporting community-level change agents like HDAs, can be applied in an integrated fashion for the malaria interventions (e.g., LLINs, IRS, early diagnosis and treatment compliance). For communications activities related to RDTs and ACTs in particular, PMI will work with health providers at different levels of the health system to strengthen their interpersonal communication skills. The SBCC strategy may follow any behavioral framework that is appropriate for the Ethiopia situation. An example of a framework that may offer a way to organize the SBCC approach is the so-called "Essential Malaria Actions" which will also supplement the SBCC activities of HDAs and HEWs.

Proposed Activities with FY 2015 Funding ($900,000):

PMI will continue to support SBCC activities to complement and support the national malaria BCC strategies. The proposed activities with FY 2015 funding are articulated to support and reinforce interpersonal communication channels to deliver malaria messages and work through a wide range of implementing partners and in-country stakeholders including HEWs and HDAs at the community level. Additionally, PMI will continue to support malaria IEC/BCC message design, production, and distribution and implement targeted SBCC activities using the most appropriate communication channels.

• **Social behavior change communication in health ($500,000):** With FY 2015 funding, PMI will continue to support the implementation of an integrated health SBCC mechanism. This mechanism was designed to build strong capacity within national and regional health bureaus, *woredas*, and Primary Health Care Units as well as local institutions, including NGOs, community-based organizations, and FBOs to plan, coordinate, manage, implement, and evaluate health SBCC programs and interventions. The activity will also execute evidence-based and coordinated social and behavior change communication activities to increase the knowledge, attitudes, and practices towards malaria prevention and control, to increase coverage and access to malaria services and of ANC services including institutional delivery, multidrug resistant tuberculosis, and PMTCT services in selected regions.

• **Community-based SBCC ($400,000):** With FY 2015 funding, PMI will continue to support two local organizations to carry out community based BCC activities in selected 10 *woredas* of both Oromia and Amhara Regions. This activity will continue to target school communities,

FBOs, and local media. This will help to reinforce and complement the HDAs community-based interpersonal behavioral change interventions.

CAPACITY BUILDING & HEALTH SYSTEMS STRENGTHENING

NMCP/PMI Objectives

Ethiopia faces many challenges related to human resources for health care, including the shortage of skilled health workers, high turnover, and lack retention of health professionals in remote and inaccessible health facilities where malaria is prevalent. Decentralization of the health care system places an additional management burden on the Regional, Zonal, and District Health Offices. While it is beyond the ability of PMI to address the system-wide capacity issues, there are areas within the NMCP and Regional Health Bureaus where capacity can be strengthened, including through pre- and in-service refresher trainings. The Ethiopian Human Resource for Health strategy aimed to develop and maintain a health workforce that is appropriately sized, skilled, well-balanced, distributed, resourced, and performing efficiently and effectively in order to provide all Ethiopians with equal access to a minimum health care package, sufficient to meet Ethiopia's health development targets in a fiscally responsible manner.

Human Resource for Health is a five-year (2012-2017),USAID-funded bilateral program to support the efforts of the Ethiopian government in improving and retaining a skilled health workforce for service delivery of key health services including malaria. The program has four key result areas:

- Improve HRH management
- Increase availability of midwives, anesthetists, HEWs, and other essential health workers
- Increase quality of health worker training
- Program learning and research

Progress During the Last 12 Months

During 2014, with the support of the USAID HRH program 3,332 midwifery, 200 anesthesia and 274 paramedics graduated from pre-service training institutions. Similarly, 1,604 health care workers also graduated from the in-service training program. In the program, generic educational standards for health worker education were developed, Health Sciences Education Development Centers in 56 universities were strengthened and supported Regional Health Science colleges. In addition, the HRH baseline survey was conducted and the HRH project monitoring tool was also developed.

The FMOH HRH Strategy was released in June 2010. PMI intends to support this strategy through supporting pre- and in-service training for HEWs, midwives, and other health care workers, to include best practices in malaria diagnosis and treatment and prevention of malaria among pregnant mothers and newborns. PMI collaborated with partners to strengthen the capacity of the ORHB and FMOH staff and others at the national, district, and community levels to plan, implement, supervise, monitor and evaluate malaria prevention and control activities.

Despite PMI and other donors' support, it was realized that the ORHB has limited capacity in human resources and has not been able to effectively coordinate with PMI implementing partners and other partners and their many malaria-related activities. The high turnover rate at FMOH and limited human resources capacities of RHBs are commonly mentioned as challenges for this effort. In addition, ORHB identified coordination of implementing partners as a major challenge. This has limited the reporting of progress of malaria control in Oromia with overlapping coverage in some areas, poor coverage in others, inadequate data sharing for partners to monitor progress, and poor utility of existing resources.

Plans and Justification

There is a need to support ORHB to improve coordination with malaria stakeholders through coordination meetings, joint planning, supportive supervision for district level program implementation, and convening public symposia to share program updates, challenges, and best practices.

Proposed Activities with FY 2015 Funding ($100,000):

• **Coordination support for ORHB ($100,000):** Support joint planning, coordination, support supervision, and review activities with all malaria stakeholders in ORHB.

• **Training and capacity building of midwives:** Please see *Malaria in Pregnancy* section under prevention portfolio for details.

STAFFING AND ADMINISTRATION

Two highly trained global health professionals serve as Resident Advisors (RAs) to oversee PMI's projects and activities in Ethiopia, one representing CDC and one representing USAID. Four Foreign Service Nationals (FSNs) were hired to support the PMI team: one Senior Malaria Advisor, one Malaria Advisor, a Malaria & HIV specialist, and one Program Manager. All PMI staff members are part of a single interagency team led by the USAID Mission Director or his/her designee in country. The PMI team shares responsibility for development and implementation of PMI strategies and work plans, coordination with national authorities, managing collaborating agencies and supervising day-to-day activities. Candidates for resident advisor positions (whether initial hires or replacements) will be evaluated and/or interviewed jointly by USAID and CDC, and both agencies will be involved in hiring decisions, with the final decision made by the individual agency.

PMI professional staff work together to oversee all technical and administrative aspects of PMI, including finalizing details of the project design, implementing malaria prevention and treatment activities, monitoring and evaluation of outcomes and impact, reporting of results, and providing guidance to PMI partners.

The PMI lead in country is the USAID/Ethiopia Mission Director. The two PMI RAs, one from USAID and one from CDC, report to the Senior USAID Health Officer for day-to-day leadership, and work together as a part of a single interagency team. The technical expertise housed in Atlanta and Washington guides PMI programmatic efforts and thus overall technical guidance for both RAs falls to PMI staff in Atlanta and Washington. Since CDC resident advisors are CDC employees (CDC USDD—38), responsibility for completing official performance reviews lies with the CDC Country Director who is expected to rely upon input from PMI staff across the two agencies that work closely day in and day out with the CDC RA and thus best positioned to comment on the RA's performance.

The two PMI resident advisors are based within the USAID health office and are expected to spend approximately half their time sitting with and providing technical assistance to the national and regional malaria control programs and partners.

Locally-hired staff to support PMI activities either in Ministries or in USAID will be approved by the USAID Mission Director. Because of the need to adhere to specific country policies and USAID accounting regulations, any transfer of PMI funds directly to Ministries or host governments will need to be approved by the USAID Mission Director and Controller, in addition to the PMI Coordinator.

Proposed Activities with FY 2015 funding ($2,150,000):

- **Management of PMI ($2,150,000):** Support to six staff members, including two senior Resident Advisors (one USAID and one CDC) and four FSNs based at the USAID Mission within the U.S. Embassy in Addis Ababa. The support includes all work-related expenses (e.g., salaries, travel, supplies, etc.), and Mission-based expenditures, including USAID Mission expenses incurred in the direct implementation of PMI activities.

Table I
President's Malaria Initiative – *Ethiopia*
Year 8 (FY 2015) Budget Breakdowns by Partner ($40,000,000)

Partner Organization	Geographic Area	Activity	Budget
APS	Oromia/National	APS for local implementation of BCC campaigns	$400,000
CDC IAA	National	In-country staff; administrative expenses, TDYs, entomology supplies and equipment; and FELTP	$632,600
G2G	National	Strengthening data management capacity, Coordination support for ORHB	$200,000
GEMS II	Oromia	Environmental monitoring	$35,000
JHPIEGO HRH	National	Expanding malaria in pregnancy services through safe motherhood and FANC	$500,000
ICAP	Oromia/National	Support for QA system for malaria laboratory diagnosis; and Therapeutic efficacy study	$1,110,000
TBD	National	Provide systems support for ongoing supervision and monitoring of malaria treatment; epidemic surveillance and response	$1,200,000
IRS 2 TO 6	Oromia/National	IRS operations; Entomological monitoring and capacity-building; and IRS national level technical assistance	$8,750,000
SIAPS	National	Strengthening of drug management system capacity	$750,000
SMMES	National	Net durability monitoring; Strengthening PHEM system and epidemic response; Operational research	$1,250,000
TBD	National	Private sector support to case management training	$300,000
TBD	National	PFSA strengthening	$250,000
TBD	National	LLIN distribution from districts to health posts	$480,000
TBD	Oromia/National	SBCC for LLINs, IRS, ACTs, case management	$500,000
UNICEF	Oromia/National	Procurement and distribution of LLINs, RDTs, laboratory equipment and supplies, ACTs, chloroquine, pre-referral and severe antimalarial drugs, primaquine; support for national commodities' micro-planning	$21,492,400
USP PQM	National	Strengthen drug quality monitoring	$400,000
USAID Staffing & Administration	National	Staffing and administration	$1,750,000
Total			$40,000,000

Table II
President's Malaria Initiative – *Ethiopia*
Planned Obligations for FY 2015 ($40,000,000)

Proposed Activity	Mechanism	Budget	Commodities	Geographic Area	Description of Activity
PREVENTION					
INSECTICIDE-TREATED BED NETS					
LLIN procurement and distribution	UNICEF	12,800,000	11,200,000	Oromia/National	Provide 3,200,000 free LLINs through health facilities, HEWs and other networks at approx. $3.50/net procurement plus $0.50/net for distribution to district.
LLIN distribution from districts to health posts	TBD	480,000		National	LLIN distribution from districts to health posts at $0.15/net.
Subtotal		*13,280,000*	*11,200,000*		
INDOOR RESIDUAL SPRAYING					
IRS operations	IRS 2 TO 6	8,250,000	4,250,000	Oromia/National	Training, implementation and supervision support for IRS operations in 26 districts; procurement of spray equipment and PPE; procurement of insecticide for IRS activities and national level technical assistance.
Entomological monitoring and capacity-building	IRS 2 TO 6	500,000		National	Sustaining capacity for entomological monitoring for vector control.
Entomological supplies and equipment	CDC IAA	10,000	10,000	National	Provide critical supplies, reagents and equipment for routine entomological monitoring activities and resistance and bionomic studies.
Entomological technical assistance	CDC IAA	36,300		National	Provide three TA visits from CDC/Atlanta for training, planning and monitoring entomological activities.
Environmental monitoring	GEMS II	35,000		Oromia	To support an independent environmental monitoring and compliance inspection for IRS.
Subtotal		*8,831,300*	*4,260,000*		
MALARIA IN PREGNANCY					
Expanding malaria in pregnancy services through safe motherhood and FANC	JHPIEGO HRH	500,000		National	Pre-service training of HEWs & midwives to ensure that malaria will be focused in pre- and in-service training for management of acute malaria in pregnant women.

Activity	Description	Location			Partner
Subtotal			500,000		
Subtotal Prevention			**22,611,300**	**15,460,000**	
CASE MANAGEMENT					
DIAGNOSIS					
Procurement of RDTs	Procurement and distribution of 5,400,000 RDTs to support FMOH/ORHB efforts to scale-up RDT use at the health facility level.	Oromia/National	3,800,000	3,800,000	UNICEF
Support for QA system for malaria laboratory diagnosis	This will include support for refresher training, supervision, other QA/QC activities, and program monitoring; training and accreditation will be provided to laboratory supervisors.	Oromia/National	1,000,000		ICAP
Procurement of laboratory equipment/supplies	Procurement of laboratory equipment and supplies (e.g., microscopes), and including logistics systems support.	Oromia	750,000	750,000	UNICEF
Subtotal			5,550,000	4,550,000	
TREATMENT					
Procurement of ACTs, chloroquine, pre-referral treatment and drugs for severe malaria, and primaquine	Procurement of 2.6 million ACTs, chloroquine, primaquine, pre-referral treatment and drugs for severe malaria.	Oromia/National	3,802,400	3,802,400	UNICEF
Provide systems support for ongoing supervision and monitoring of malaria treatment	Support for health worker supervision for management of malaria at district-level health centers and community-level health posts; collaboration with Zonal and District Health Offices; iCCM.	National	1,000,000		TBD
Private sector support to case management training	Work with the RHBs and private health facilities in Amhara and Oromia to increase access to quality malaria services.	Amhara & Oromia	300,000		TBD
Subtotal			5,102,400	3,802,400	
PHARMACEUTICAL MANAGEMENT					
Strengthening of drug management system capacity	Strengthening of drug management system, quantification and procurement; distribution management; and health facility drug availability.	National	750,000	750,000	SIAPS